Editor
Sara Connolly

Illustrator
Howard Chaney

Cover Artist
Brenda DiAntonis

Managing Editor
Karen J. Goldfluss, M.S. Ed.

Creative Director
Karen J. Goldfluss, M.S. Ed.

Art Production Manager
Kevin Barnes

Art Coordinator
Renée Christine Yates

Imaging
Denise Thomas
James Edward Grace
Nathan Rivera

Publisher
Mary D. Smith, M.S. Ed.

The classroom teacher may reproduce copies of materials in this book for classroom use only. Reproduction of any part for an entire school or school system is strictly prohibited. No part of this publication may be transmitted, stored, or recorded in any form without written permission from the publisher.

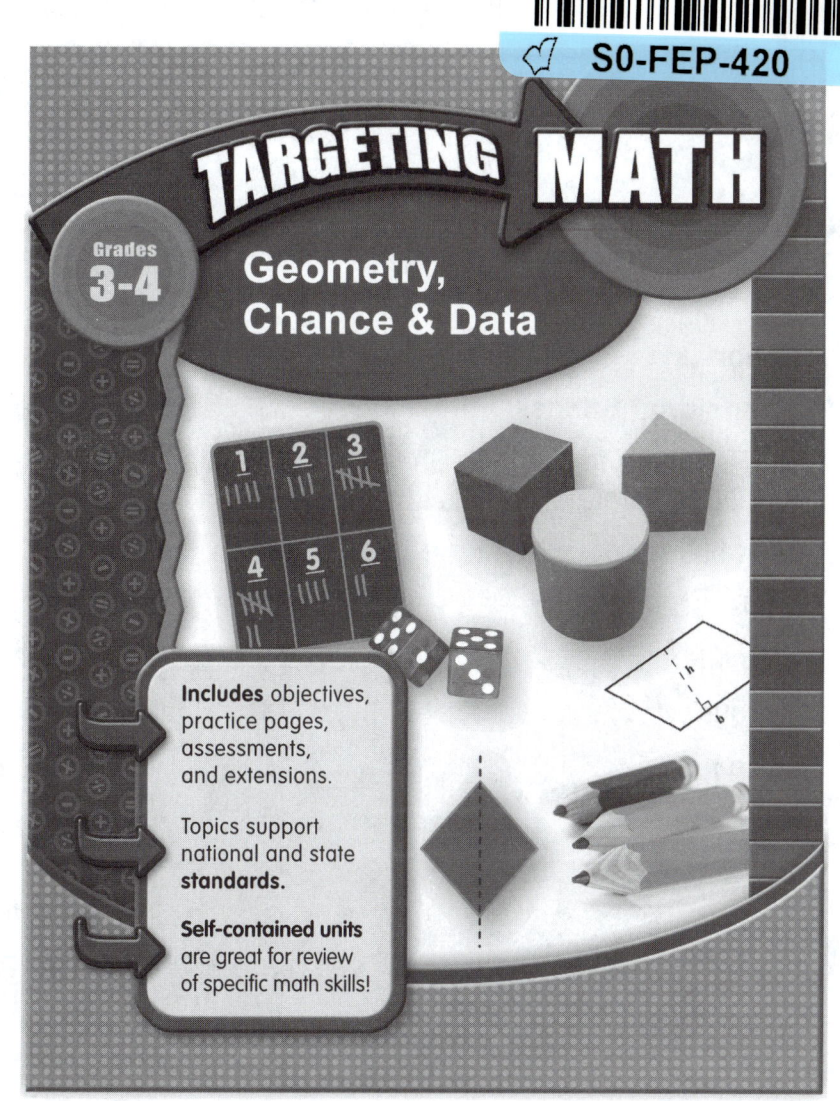

Authors

Jo Grinham, Dona Martin, and Angela Toohey

(Revised and Rewritten by Teacher Created Resources, Inc.)

Teacher Created Resources, Inc.
6421 Industry Way
Westminster, CA 92683
www.teachercreated.com
ISBN: 978-1-4206-8995-2

© 2007 Teacher Created Resources, Inc.
Reprinted, 2008
Made in U.S.A.

Table of Contents

Introduction 4
Two-Dimensional Shapes 5
   Unit 1: Regular and Irregular Shapes, and Quadrilaterals 6
      Shape Names 8
      Regular and Irregular 9
      Quadrilaterals 10
      Polygons 11
      Angles 12
      Drawing Angles 13
      Assessment 14
      Activity Page 15
   Unit 2: Angles, Symmetry, Patterns, Making Shapes, and Parallel Lines 16
      Angles 18
      Axes of Symmetry 19
      Naming Angles 20
      Tessellations 21
      Making Shapes 22
      Parallel Lines 23
      Assessment 24
Three-Dimensional Shapes 25
   Unit 1: Naming, Cross-Sections, Drawing, Faces, Edges, and Corners 26
      Identifying Objects 28
      Pyramids 29
      Naming Geometric Solids 30
      Three-Dimensional Chart 31
      Cross-Sections 32
      Three-Dimensional Objects 33

Assessment 34
Activity Page 35
   Unit 2: Drawing, Prisms, Cross-Sections, Views, and Unfolded Figures 36
      Drawing Objects 38
      Prisms 39
      Cross-Sections 40
      Completing Three-Dimensional Drawings 41
      Bases 42
      Views 43
      Assessment 44
Position, Mapping, Transformation, and Symmetry 45
   Unit 1: Position and Mapping 46
      Simple Directions 48
      Following Directions 49
      Reading Maps 50
      Position on Maps 51
      Map Coordinates 52
      Basic Geography 53
      Assessment 54
      Activity Page 55
   Unit 2: Transformation and Symmetry . . . 56
      Flip, Slide, and Turn 58
      Tangrams 59
      Lines of Symmetry 60
      Symmetry 61
      More Lines of Symmetry 62

#8995 Targeting Math: Geometry, Chance and Data   © Teacher Created Resources, Inc.

Table of Contents

    Patterns 63
    Assessment 64
    Activity Pages 65

Graphs 67
Unit 1: Recording Information,
    Tally Marks, Picture Graphs, Column
    Graphs, and Problem Solving 68
    Tally Marks 70
    Picture Graph 71
    Column Graph 72
    Problem Solving 73
    Line Graph 74
    Bar Graph 75
    Assessment 76
    Activity Page 77
Unit 2: Surveys, Tally, Picture Graph, Bar
    Graphs, Line Graphs, and Picture
    Graphs 78
    Traffic Survey 80
    Picture Graph 81
    Bar Graphs 82
    More Graphs 83
    Pie Graphs 84
    Line Graphs 85
    Assessment 86

Chance and Data 87
Unit 1: Chance. Probabbility, Certainty,
    Possible, Impossible, Likely, and
    Unlikely Combinations 88

    Possibility 90
    Possible Paths 91
    True or False 92
    Being Certain 93
    Chances 94
    Choices! Choices! 95
    Assessment 96
    Activity Page 97
Unit 2: Data, Predictions, Chance, and
    Experiments 98
    Funny Faces 100
    Most Likely 101
    Predictions 102
    Chance 103
    Different Ways 104
    Tossing Coins 105
    Assessment 106

Unfolded Figures 107
    The Cube 107
    The Triangular Prism 108
    The Cylinder 109
    The Cone 110

Skills Index 111

© Teacher Created Resources, Inc.   #8995 Targeting Math: Geometry, Chance and Data

Introduction

Targeting Math

The series *Targeting Math* is a comprehensive classroom resource. It has been developed so that teachers can find activities and reproducible pages for all areas of the primary math curriculum.

About This Series

The twelve books in the series cover all aspects of the math curriculum in an easy to access format. Each level—grades 1 and 2, grades 3 and 4, and grades 5 and 6—has four books: *Numeration and Fractions*; *Operations and Number Patterns*; *Geometry, Chance, and Data*; and *Measurement*. Each topic in the book is covered by one or more units that are progressive in level. You will be able to find resources for each student, whatever his or her ability may be. This enables you to differentiate for different ability groups within your class. It also allows you to quickly find worksheets at different levels for remediation and extension.

About This Book

Targeting Math: Geometry, Chance, and Data (Grades 3 and 4) contains topics covering Two-Dimensional Shapes; Three-Dimensional Shapes; Position, Mapping, and Transformation; Graphs; and Chance and Data. Each topic is covered by two complete units of work. (See Table of Contents for specific skills.)

About Each Unit

Each unit is complete within itself. It begins with a list of objectives, resources needed, mathematical language used, and a description of each reproducible. This is followed by suggested student activities to reinforce learning. The reproducible pages cover different aspects of the topic in a progressive nature and all answers are included. Every unit includes an assessment page. These assessment pages are important resources in themselves as teachers can use them to find out what their students know about a new topic. They can also be used for assessing specific outcomes when clear feedback is needed.

About the Skills Index

A Skills Index is provided at the end of the book. It lists specific objectives for the student pages of each unit of the book.

#8995 Targeting Math: Geometry, Chance and Data © Teacher Created Resources, Inc.

TWO-DIMENSIONAL SHAPES

These units provide opportunities to name, classify, and draw two-dimensional shapes. Students identify regular and irregular shapes; acute, obtuse, straight and right angles; axes of symmetry; parallel lines; and quadrilaterals.

Students practice skills with patterns, tessellations, parallel lines, and symmetry. Two assessment pages are included. Also included is an activity page in which two-dimensional shapes are manipulated to form numbers.

© Teacher Created Resources, Inc. #8995 Targeting Math: Geometry, Chance and Data

TWO-DIMENSIONAL SHAPES

Unit 1
**Regular and Irregular Shapes
Quadrilaterals**

Objectives
- make, classify, name, and describe the properties of two-dimensional shapes
- appreciate the importance of visualization when problem-solving
- recognize, name, make, and describe the properties of simple two-dimensional shapes using everyday language by observing similarities and differences
- demonstrate in practical situations that an angle is an amount of rotation and describe and compare angles using everyday language

Language
square, triangle, rectangle, rhombus, pentagon, hexagon, two-dimensional, octagon, pattern, irregular, quadrilateral, sides, corners, angle, obtuse, acute, straight, right angle, curved edge

Materials/Resources
ruler, blank paper, colored pencils, cardboard

Contents of Student Pages
* Materials needed for each reproducible student page

Page 8 Shape Names
naming shapes; drawing shapes
* colored pencils

Page 9 Regular and Irregular
regular and irregular shapes; drawing given shapes on grid paper
* colored pencils

Page 10 Quadrilaterals
recognizing quadrilaterals; rhombus patterns
* colored pencils

Page 11 Polygons
polygons—drawing, naming, sides and corners

Page 12 Angles
angles—acute angle, obtuse angle, right angle, straight angle; ordering angles

Page 13 Drawing Angles
naming angles—acute, obtuse, or right angle

Page 14 Assessment
* colored pencils

Page 15 Activity
manipulating shapes to form a number

Remember

Before starting, ensure that each student:
❑ is encouraged to check answers.
❑ uses a ruler when drawing polygons.

#8995 Targeting Math: Geometry, Chance and Data © Teacher Created Resources, Inc.

Additional Activities
- Have students trace the shapes of tangrams and make images from them. Tangrams also come in plastic form. These are excellent puzzle-making materials.
- Have students cut out polygons in colored paper and make a collage picture.
- Collect shapes from magazines and make a class chart.
- Play Shape Bingo.
- Have students work in groups of three to go on shape hunts in the playground. They should record the names of the shapes and where they were found.

Answers
Page 8 Shape Names
1. Check individual work.
2. a. triangle
   b. square
   c. rectangle
   d. octagon
   e. pentagon
   f. rhombus

Page 9 Regular and Irregular
1. Check individual work.
2. Irregular shapes—a, b, f, g, h
   Regular shapes—c, d, e, i

Page 10 Quadrilaterals
1. Check individual work.
2. Quadrilaterals—a, b, e, g, i, k, l

Page 11 Polygons
square	4, 4
circle	1, 0
triangle	3, 3
pentagon	5, 5
octagon	8, 8
hexagon	6, 6
parallelogram	4, 4
rectangle	4, 4
decagon	10, 10
rhombus	4, 4

Page 12 Angles
1. a. obtuse
   b. acute
   c. straight
   d. right
   e. acute
   f. obtuse
   g. right
   h. straight
   i. obtuse
   j. straight
   k. acute
   l. obtuse
2. h(1), i(2), g(3), f(4), j(5), e(6), a(7), b(8), c(9), d(10)

Page 13 Drawing Angles
1. Check individual work.
2. Check individual work.

Page 14 Assessment
1. a. acute
   b. right angle
   c. straight
   d. obtuse
2. a. triangle
   b. square
   c. rhombus
   d. hexagon
   e. rectangle
3. Irregular—a, c, e
   Regular—b, d
4. Check individual work.
5. a. 6
   b. pentagon
   c. circle
   d. 4

6. a.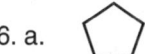

   b. Check individual work.

Page 15 Activity Page

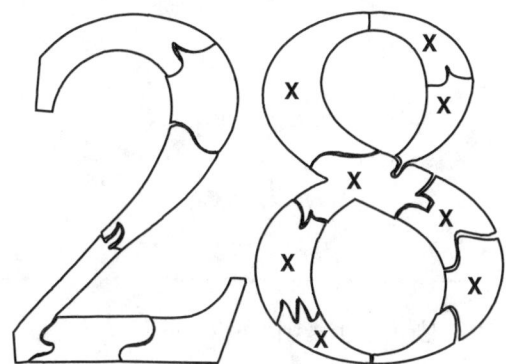

© Teacher Created Resources, Inc.   #8995 Targeting Math: Geometry, Chance and Data

Two-Dimensional Shapes　　　　　　　　　　　　　　　　　　　　　Shape Names

Name　　　　　　　　　　　　　　　　　　　　**Date**

1. Draw a line from each shape to its name.

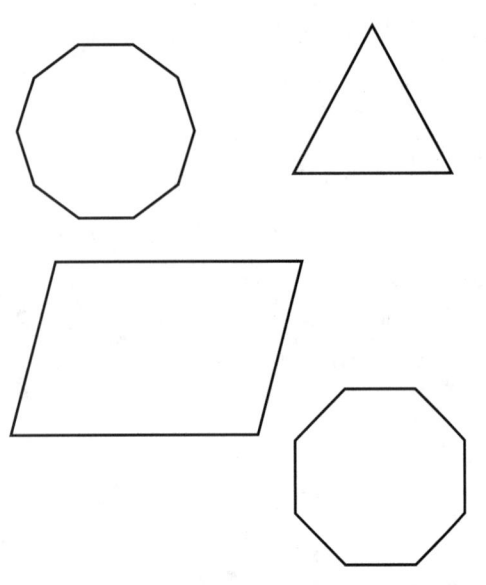

square

triangle

pentagon

hexagon

decagon

rhombus

rectangle

octagon

circle

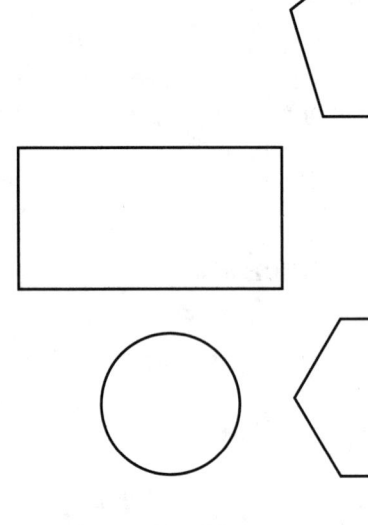

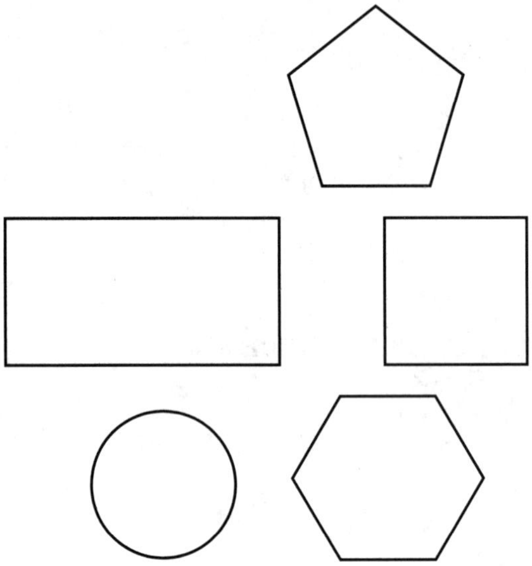

2. Connect the numbers to make each two-dimensional shape. Write the name of each shape on the line below it.

a.　　　　　　　　　　　　　b.　　　　　　　　　　　　　c.

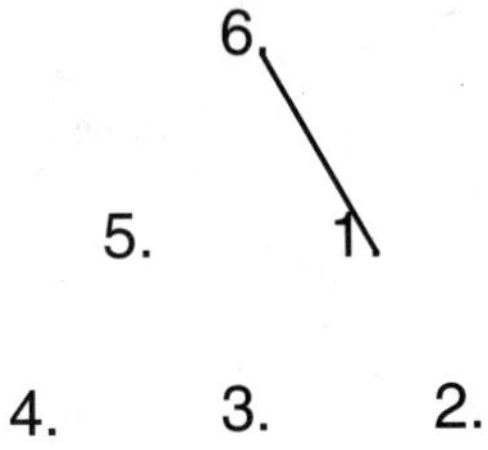

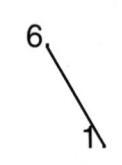　　　　　　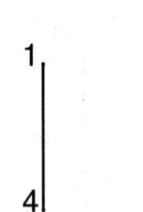　　　　　　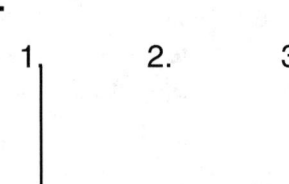

_____　　　_____　　　_____

d.　　　　　　　　　　　　　e.　　　　　　　　　　　　　f.

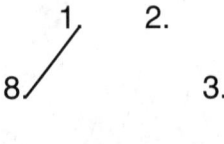　　　　　　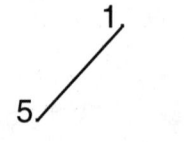　　　　　　

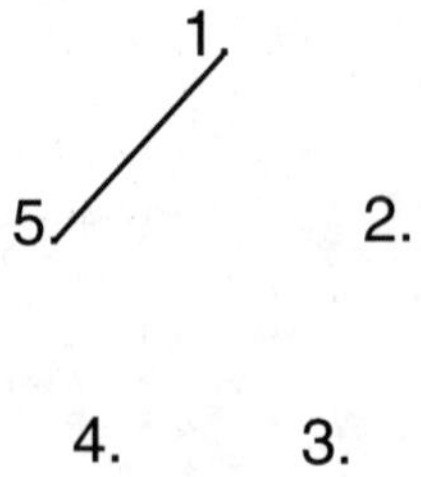

_____　　　_____　　　_____

g. Color the triangle blue.

h. Make a checkmark inside the square.

i. Draw a pattern on the octagon.

j. Put a star on the rectangle.

#8995 Targeting Math: Geometry, Chance and Data　　　　　© Teacher Created Resources, Inc.

Two-Dimensional Shapes   Regular and Irregular

Name   **Date**

1. In the box below, draw the following polygons.

   square

   hexagon

   pentagon

   rhombus

   triangle

2. Color the irregular shapes red and the regular shapes blue.

   a.  b. 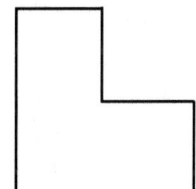 c.

   d. 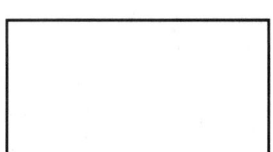 e.  f.

   g.  h. 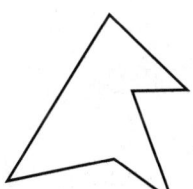 i.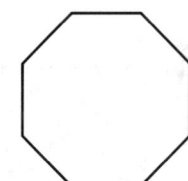

© Teacher Created Resources, Inc.   #8995 Targeting Math: Geometry, Chance and Data

Two-Dimensional Shapes   Quadrilaterals

Name   **Date**

1. Use four different colors to create a pattern with these rhombus shapes.

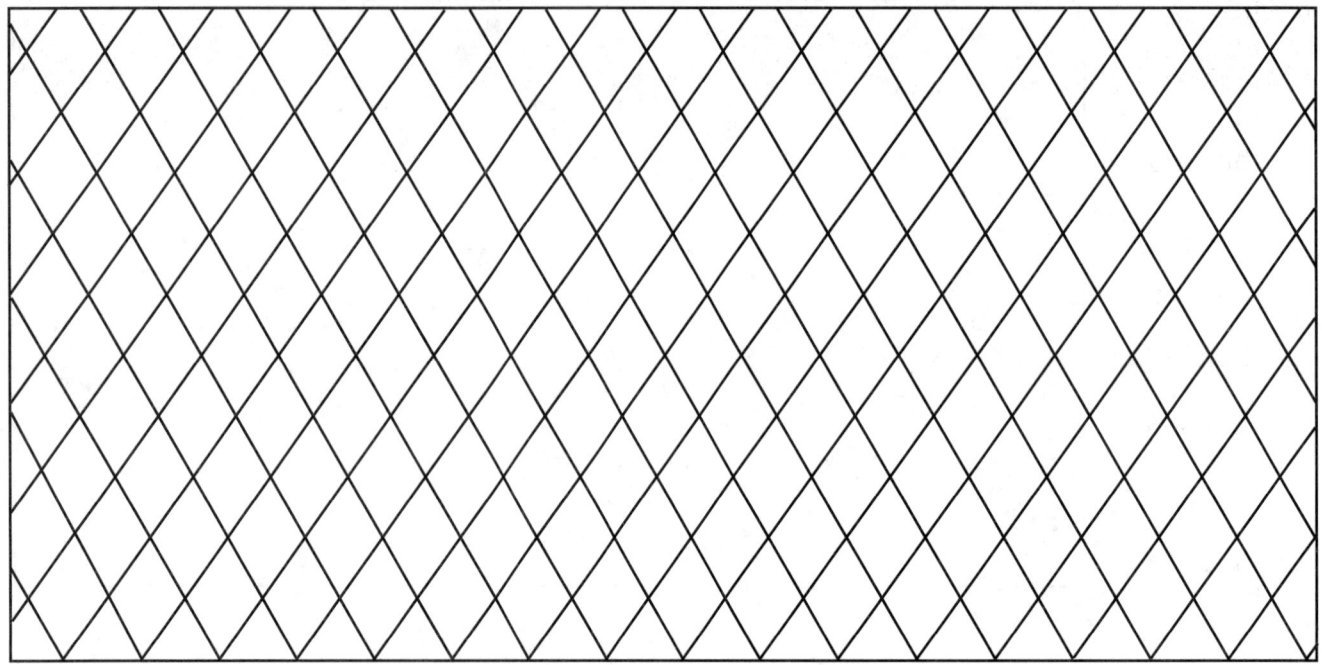

2. Quadrilaterals are shapes that have four sides. Color all the quadrilaterals.

a. 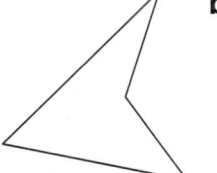 b.  c. 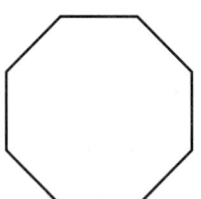 d.

e. 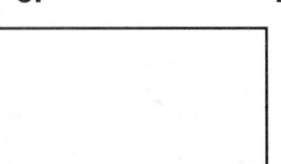 f. 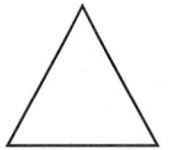 g. 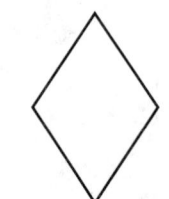 h.

i. 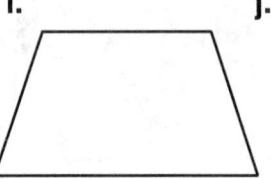 j. 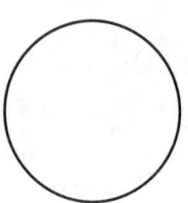 k. 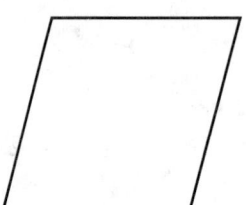 l.

#8995 Targeting Math: Geometry, Chance and Data   © Teacher Created Resources, Inc.

Two-Dimensional Shapes   *Polygons*

Name   **Date**

Complete the chart.

Shape	Name	Your Drawing	Number of Sides	Number of Corners
☐ square				
○ circle				
△ triangle				
⬠ pentagon				
⯃ octagon				
⬡ hexagon				
▱ rhombus				
▭ rectangle				
◯ decagon				
◇ diamond				

© Teacher Created Resources, Inc.   #8995 Targeting Math: *Geometry, Chance and Data*

Two-Dimensional Shapes   *Angles*

Name   **Date**

1. Use the corner of a book to help you label these angles as obtuse, acute, right, or straight angles.

a. 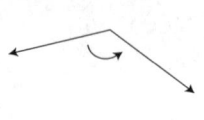   b. 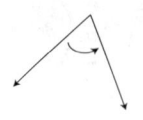   c. 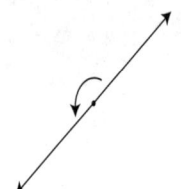   d.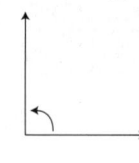

e. 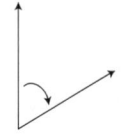   f. 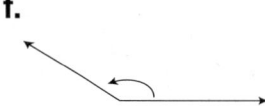   g. 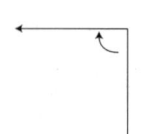   h.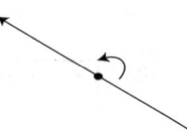

i. 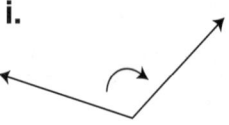   j. 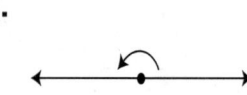   k. 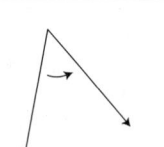   l.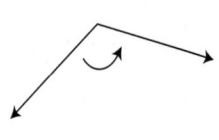

2. Label these angles 1 to 10, from the most obtuse to the most acute.

a. 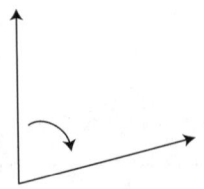   b.   c.   d.   e.

f.   g. 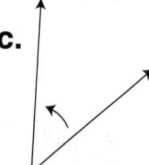   h. 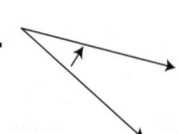   i. 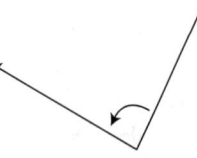   j.

 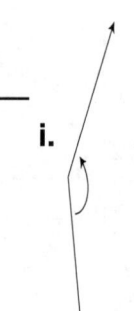 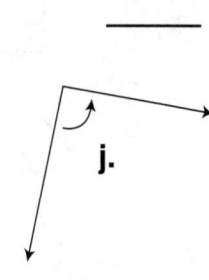

12

#8995 *Targeting Math: Geometry, Chance and Data*   © *Teacher Created Resources, Inc.*

Two-Dimensional Shapes   Drawing Angles

Name   **Date**

1. Draw four different angles on the grids and then name them.

   a.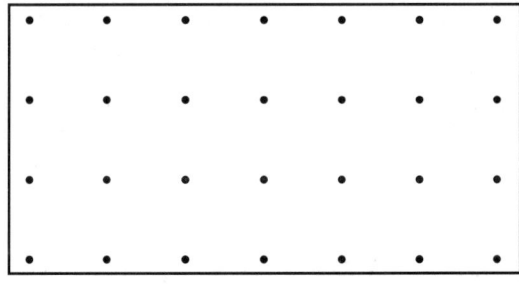

   _____ angle

   b.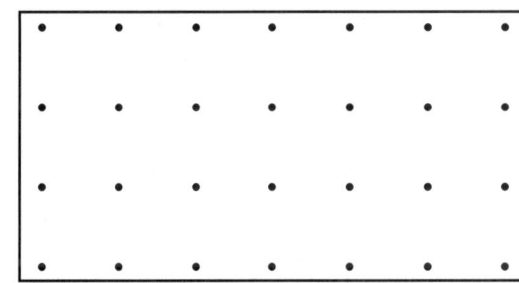

   _____ angle

   c.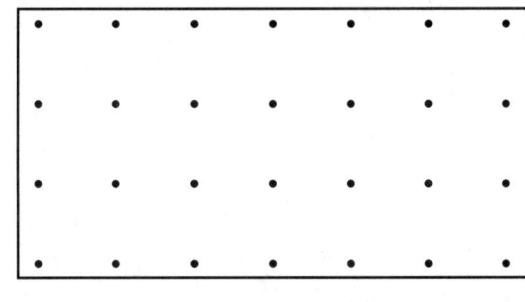

   _____ angle

   d.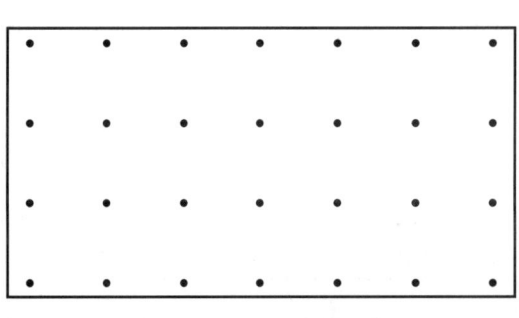

   _____ angle

2. Look at these shapes. Inside the shapes, label each angle **O** for obtuse, **A** for acute, and **R** for right angle.

   a. 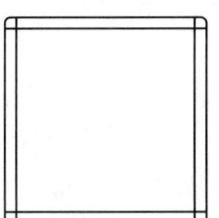   b. 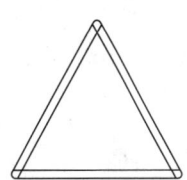   c.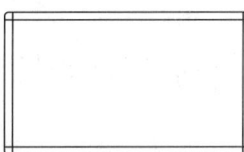

   d.    e. 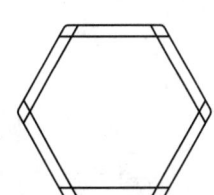   f.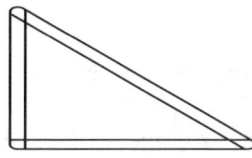

   g. 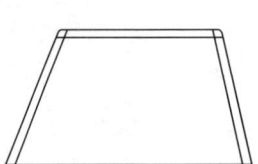 h. 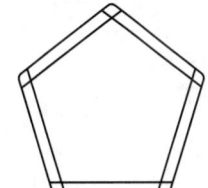 i.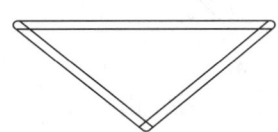

© Teacher Created Resources, Inc.   #8995 Targeting Math: Geometry, Chance and Data

Two-Dimensional Shapes Assessment

Name **Date**

1. Name these angles.

   a. 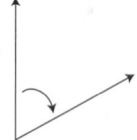   b.    c. 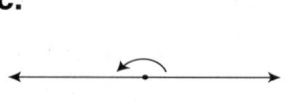   d.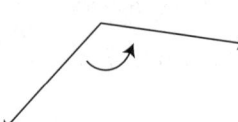

   _____   _____   _____   _____

2. Name these shapes.

   a. 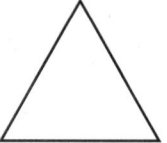   b.    c.    d. 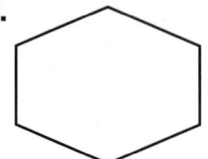   e.

   _____ _____ _____ _____ _____

3. Color the irregular shapes red and cross out the regular shapes.

   a. 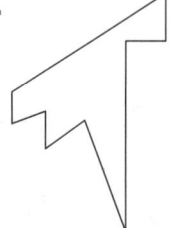   b. 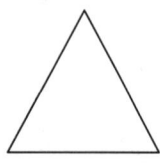   c. 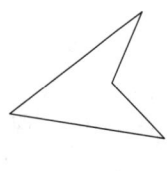   d. 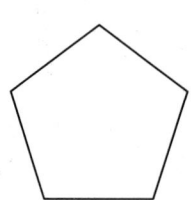   e.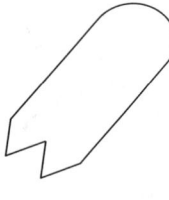

4. Draw four different quadrilaterals.

   a.   b.   c.   d.

5. Complete these sentences.

   a. A hexagon has _____ sides.   b. A _____ has 5 sides.

   c. A _____ has a curved edges.   d. A square has _____ right angles.

6. Draw:

   a. a pentagon   b. a triangle with an obtuse angle.

14

#8995 Targeting Math: Geometry, Chance and Data   © Teacher Created Resources, Inc.

Two-Dimensional Shapes   Activity Page

Name   **Date**

Where Do I Live?

Can you figure out what my house number is?

Here are some clues: It is a two-digit number.

It is not an odd number.

Cut out the puzzle pieces below and arrange them to make my house number. The pieces with Xs on them belong together and make up the second digit.

TWO-DIMENSIONAL SHAPES

Unit 2

Angles
Symmetry
Patterns
Making Shapes
Parallel Lines

Objectives

- recognize, name and make simple two-dimensional shapes and describe their properties using everyday language by observing similarities and differences
- make, classify, name, and describe the properties of two-dimensional geometrical shapes
- demonstrate in practical situations that an angle is an amount of rotation and describe and compare angles using everyday language
- appreciate the importance of visualization when problem solving
- create tessellations and other patterns

Language

square, circle, triangle, rectangle, rhombus, pentagon, hexagon, octagon, decagon, angles, acute, obtuse, straight, right angle

Materials/Resources

ruler, blank paper, colored pencils, cardboard

Contents of Student Pages

* Materials needed for each reproducible student page

Page 18 Angles
acute, obtuse, straight and right angles

Page 19 Axes of Symmetry
naming shapes; drawing axes of symmetry; completing symmetrical drawings
* colored pencils

Page 20 Naming Angles
drawing and identifying angles
* colored pencils

Page 21 Tessellations
tessellations; creating tessellating patterns; recognizing tessellation patterns
* colored pencils

Page 22 Making Shapes
using cardboard or other materials to make angles and quadrilaterals
* cardboard or plastic strips

Page 23 Parallel Lines
drawing a given shape; recognizing parallel lines

Page 24 Assessment

Remember

Before starting, ensure that each student:
- ❑ is encouraged to check answers.
- ❑ uses a ruler when drawing polygons, angles, and straight lines.

#8995 Targeting Math: Geometry, Chance and Data   © Teacher Created Resources, Inc.

Additional Activities
- Have students work in pairs. Have one student draw one side of a picture and the other draw the symmetrical image.
- Ask students to find two-dimensional shapes around the classroom.
- Do a parallel-line search in the classroom and on the playground.
- Find pictures of tessellating patterns to make a display chart.
- Find groups of objects which do/do not have an axis of symmetry.

Answers
Page 18 Angles
1. Check individual work.
2. a. right
   b. obtuse
   c. acute
   d. acute
   e. acute
   f. obtuse
3. Check individual work.

Page 19 Axes of Symmetry
1. a. triangle
   b. square
   c. rectangle
   d. octagon
   e. trapezoid
   f. hexagon
   g. circle
   h. rhombus
   i. pentagon
2. Check individual axes of symmetry.

Page 20 Naming Angles
Check individual work.

Page 21 Tessellations
1. Check individual work.
2. b and c tessellate.
3. Check individual work.

Page 22 Making Shapes
1. a. – f. Check individual work; g. b., d., f.
2. a and c, b and h, d and f, g and i, e and j

Page 23 Parallel Lines
1. Check individual work.
2. a and d
3. Check individual work.

Page 24 Assessment
1. a. square
   b. rectangle
   c. triangle
   d. hexagon
Check individual axes of symmetry.
2. Check individual work.
3. b and c
4. Check individual work.

Two-Dimensional Shapes   Angles

Name   **Date**

1. Look at these shapes.
    a. Draw a circle around all the obtuse angles.
    b. Put a checkmark on all the right angles.
    c. Cross out all the acute angles.

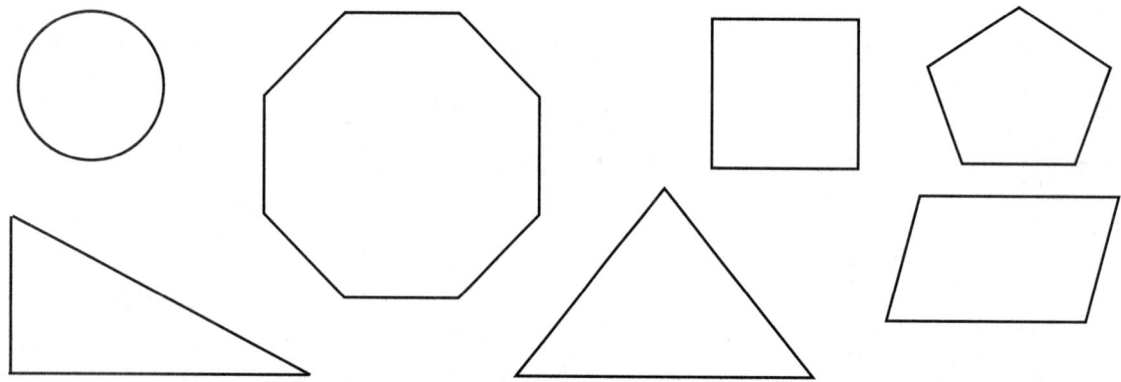

2. On the line below each angle, write whether it is an acute, obtuse, or right angle.

   a. 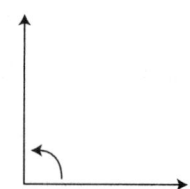   b. 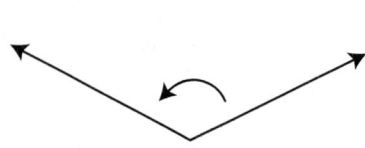   c.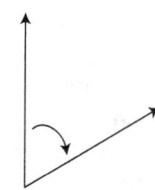

   _____   _____   _____

   d. 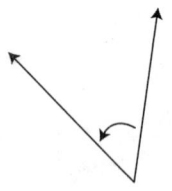   e. 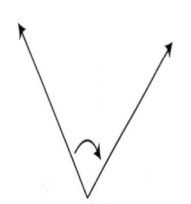   f.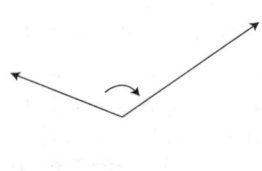

   _____   _____   _____

3. Draw and label an acute angle, an obtuse angle, and a right angle.
    a.   b.   c.

18

#8995 Targeting Math: Geometry, Chance and Data   © Teacher Created Resources, Inc.

Two-Dimensional Shapes   Axes of Symmetry

Name   **Date**

1. Name these shapes and draw the axes of symmetry for each one.

   a. 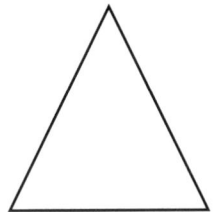   b.    c.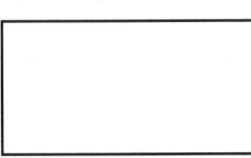

   _____   _____   _____

   d. 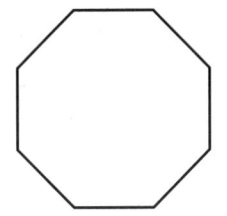   e. 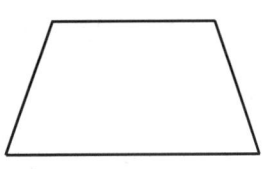   f.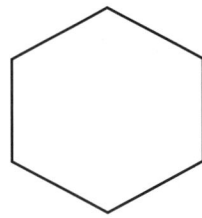

   _____   _____   _____

   g. 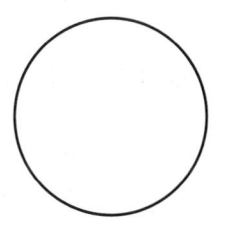   h. 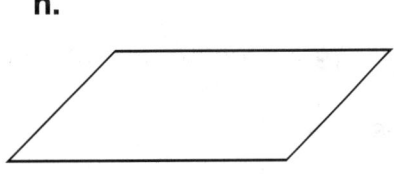   i.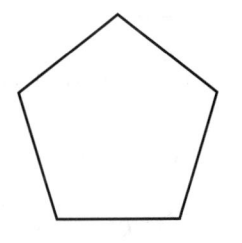

   _____   _____   _____

2. Draw the other half of each shape so that it is perfectly symmetrical. Then color the shape.

   a.    b.    c. 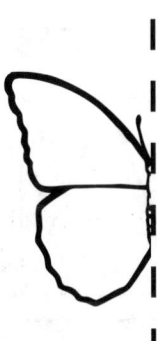   d.

© Teacher Created Resources, Inc.   #8995 Targeting Math: Geometry, Chance and Data

Two-Dimensional Shapes   Naming Angles

Name   **Date**

1. Use a ruler and the grid dots to copy each of the angles drawn.

   a. 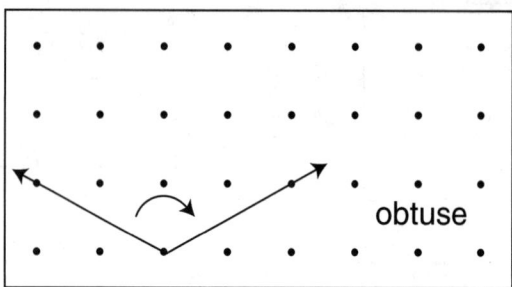 obtuse

   b. 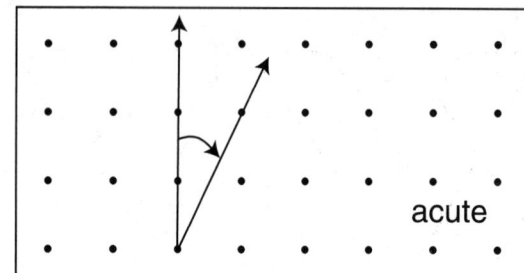 acute

   c. 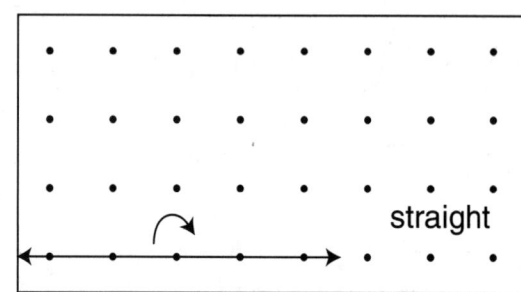 straight

   d. 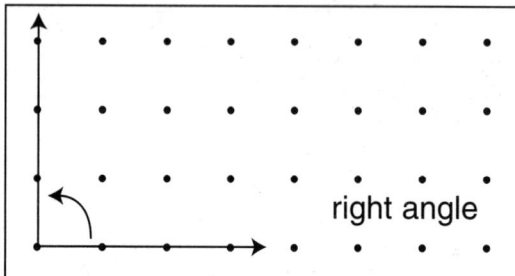 right angle

2. Look at the angles in this picture.

   a. Color the obtuse angles blue.

   b. Color the acute angles red.

   c. Color the right angles yellow.

#8995 Targeting Math: Geometry, Chance and Data   © Teacher Created Resources, Inc.

Two-Dimensional Shapes   Tessellations

| **Name** | **Date** |

1. Use three different colors to create a tessellating pattern with these rhombus shapes.

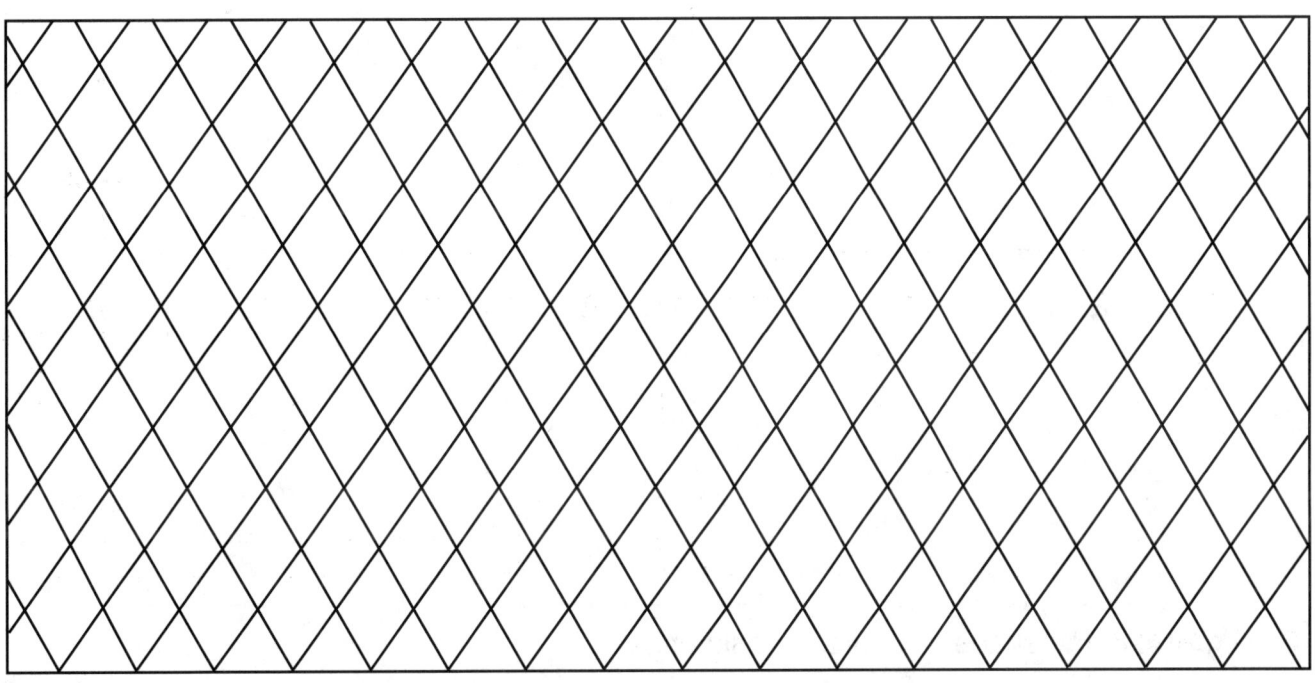

2. The pattern above is a pattern that tessellates. Color the patterns below that tessellate.

   a.   b.   c.

   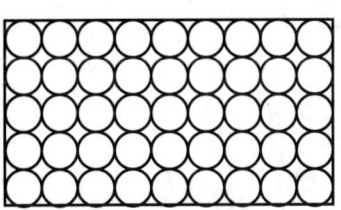   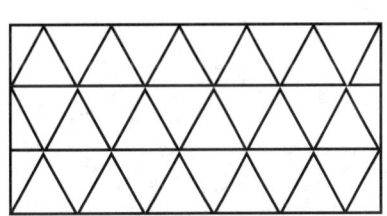   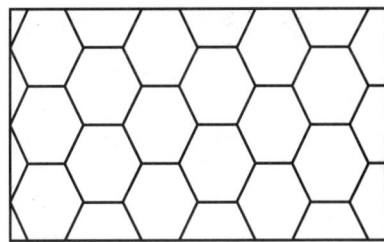

3. Draw a tessellating pattern.

Two-Dimensional Shapes   Making Shapes

Name   **Date**

1. Make each of these shapes using plastic or cardboard strips. Name each shape and label inside the shape whether the angles are **o** (obtuse), **a** (acute), or **r** (right angles).

   a.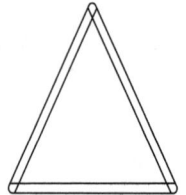

   b.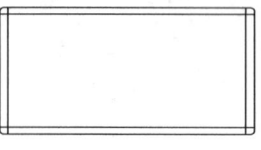

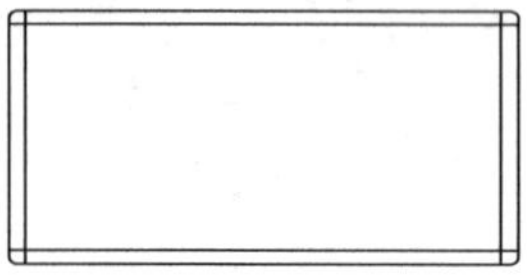

   c.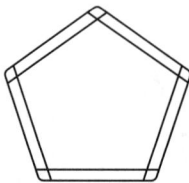

   _____   _____   _____

   d.

   e.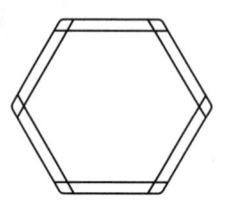

   f.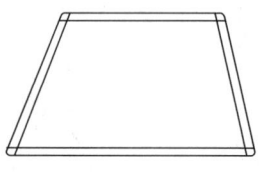

   _____   _____   _____

   g. Color the shapes that are quadrilaterals.

2. Draw lines to connect angles that are the same.

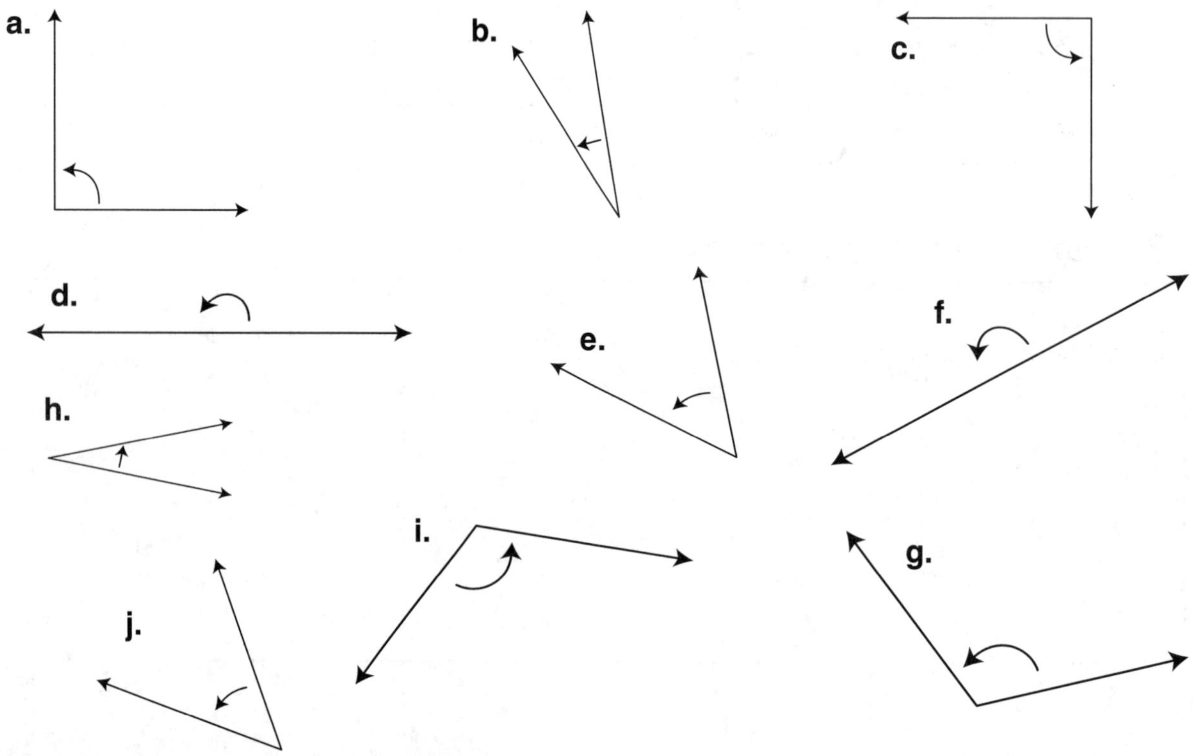

   a.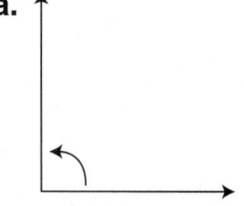

   b.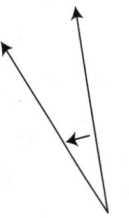

   c.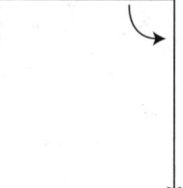

   d.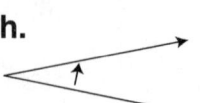

   f.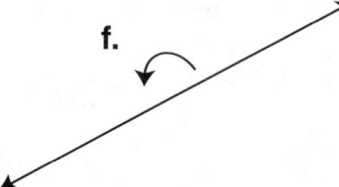

   e.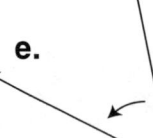

   h.

   i.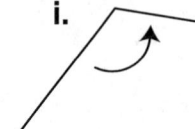

   g.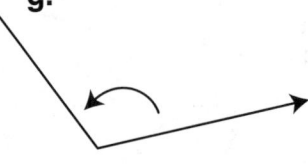

   j.

22

#8995 Targeting Math: Geometry, Chance and Data   © Teacher Created Resources, Inc.

Two-Dimensional Shapes   Parallel Lines

Name   **Date**

1. Draw:

a. a rectangle	b. a right angle	c. a hexagon
d. a triangle	e. a pentagon	f. an acute angle

2. Circle the lines that are parallel.

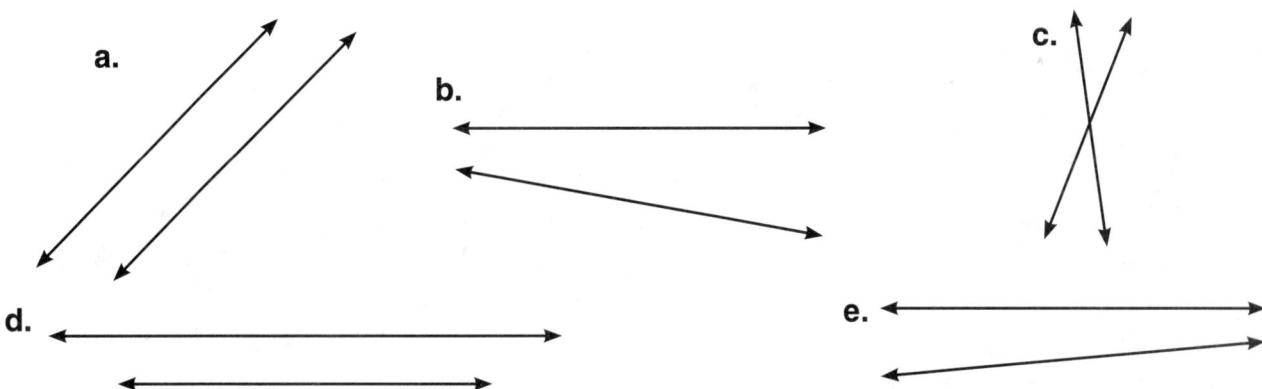

3. Draw three different sets of parallel lines.

© Teacher Created Resources, Inc.   #8995 Targeting Math: Geometry, Chance and Data

Two-Dimensional Shapes   Assessment

Name   **Date**

1. Name these shapes and draw their axes of symmetry.

   a.    b.    c. 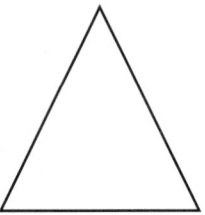   d.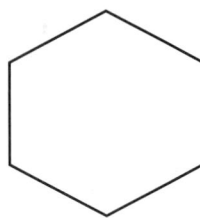

   _____   _____   _____   _____

2. Draw:

   a. a pentagon   b. a circle   c. a trapezoid   d. an octagon

   e. an acute angle   f. an obtuse angle   g. a straight angle   h. a right angle

3. Color the patterns that tessellate.

   a. 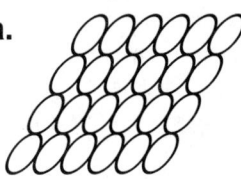   b. 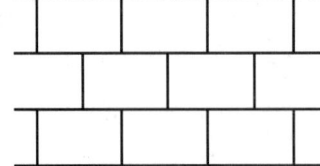   c.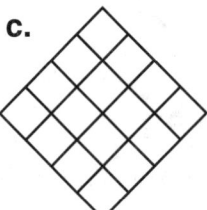

4. Look at the pattern below.
   a. Color four obtuse angles blue.
   b. Color four acute angles yellow.
   c. Circle four right angles.
   d. Draw an arrow on three lines that are parallel.

#8995 Targeting Math: Geometry, Chance and Data   © Teacher Created Resources, Inc.

THREE-DIMENSIONAL SHAPES

In these units, students explore three-dimensional shapes through naming, labeling, classifying, and drawing. They identify prisms, pyramids, faces, edges, corners and cross-sections.

Students practice skills by completing diagrams of three-dimensional shapes, patterning, and identifying unfolded figures.

The activity page contains instructions for two models which students can build in order to answer the questions.

Two assessment pages are included.

© Teacher Created Resources, Inc.

#8995 Targeting Math: Geometry, Chance and Data

THREE-DIMENSIONAL SHAPES

Unit 1
Naming
Cross-sections
Drawing
Faces
Edges
Corners

Objectives
- identify, compare, classify and construct three-dimensional objects and represent them in drawings
- describe, model, sort, and recognize three-dimensional objects using everyday language
- identify and describe prisms and pyramids
- describe and compare the spatial features of mathematical objects

Language
three-dimensional object, edge, face, corner, flat, curved, base apex, cube, prism, pyramid, cylinder, cone, sphere, triangular, rectangular, hexagonal, pentagonal, cross-section

Materials/Resources
ruler, blank paper, colored pencils, three-dimensional objects made of wood (optional, but can be very helpful)

Contents of Student Pages
* Materials needed for each reproducible student page

Page 28 Identifying Objects
curved and flat surfaces; drawing objects
* colored pencils

Page 29 Pyramids
looking at bases; drawing faces

Page 30 Naming Geometric Solids
comparing prisms and pyramids; faces, bases, edges, and corners
* colored pencils

Page 31 Three-Dimensional Chart
naming; counting faces, edges, and corners

Page 32 Cross-Sections
drawing cross-sections; drawing three-dimensional objects from clues

Page 33 Three-Dimensional Objects
drawing; naming; identifying
* colored pencils

Page 34 Assessment

Page 35 Activity
building models

Remember
Before starting, ensure that each student:
- ❑ develops the habit of checking all answers.
- ❑ uses a ruler when constructing three-dimensional objects.

#8995 Targeting Math: Geometry, Chance and Data © Teacher Created Resources, Inc.

Additional Activities

- ❏ Have students make three-dimensional objects from some form of modeling clay.
- ❏ Have students play Three-Dimensional Bingo.
- ❏ Students can make constructions using small wooden cubes. Their partners can then count how many cubes have been used.
- ❏ Find pictures of three-dimensional objects and use them to make class charts.
- ❏ Conduct a class three-dimensional hunt in the playground. Give clues as for a treasure hunt. The winners are the groups which find all objects first.
- ❏ Have students cut out and assemble the unfolded figures on pages 107–110.

Answers

Page 28 Identifying Objects
1. a. Check individual work.
   b. curved surface—sphere, cone, cylinder
   c. flat surfaces—cube, square pyramid, and rectangular prism
2. Check individual work.
3. Check individual work.

Page 29 Pyramids
1. Check individual work.
2. Check individual work.

Page 30 Naming Geometric Solids
1. a. cylinder
   b. triangular prism
   c. square pyramid
   d. cone
   e. cube
   f. rectangular pyramid
   g. octagonal prism
   h. prisms are b, e, g
   i. pyramids are c, f
2. Check individual work.

Page 31 Three-Dimensional Chart

	Shape	Name	Number of Faces	Number of Edges	Number of Corners
a.		cube	6	12	8
b.		cylinder	3	2	0
c.		triangular pyramid	4	6	4
d.		rectangular pyramid	5	8	5
e.		square pyramid	5	8	5
f.		triangular prism	5	9	6
g.		cone	2	1	0
h.		sphere	1	0	0

Page 32 Cross-Sections
1. Check individual work.
2. Check individual work.

Page 33 Three-Dimensional Objects
1. Check individual work.
2. Check individual work.

Page 34 Assessment
1. a. cube
   b. sphere
   c. triangular pyramid
   d. cone
   e. cylinder
   f. triangular prism
   g. square pyramid
   h. rectangular prism
2. prisms are a, e, f, h
3. a. 5 8 5
   b. 3 2 0
   c. 6 12 8
   d. 5 9 6
   e. 2 1 0
   f. 8 18 12
4. a. Check individual work.
   b. Check individual work.

Page 35 Activity Page
1. a. David 8, Joanna 4
   b. 216
   c. 204
   d. Check individual work.
2. Check individual work.

Three-Dimensional Shapes   Identifying Objects

Name   **Date**

1. a. Draw lines to connect the shapes to their names.

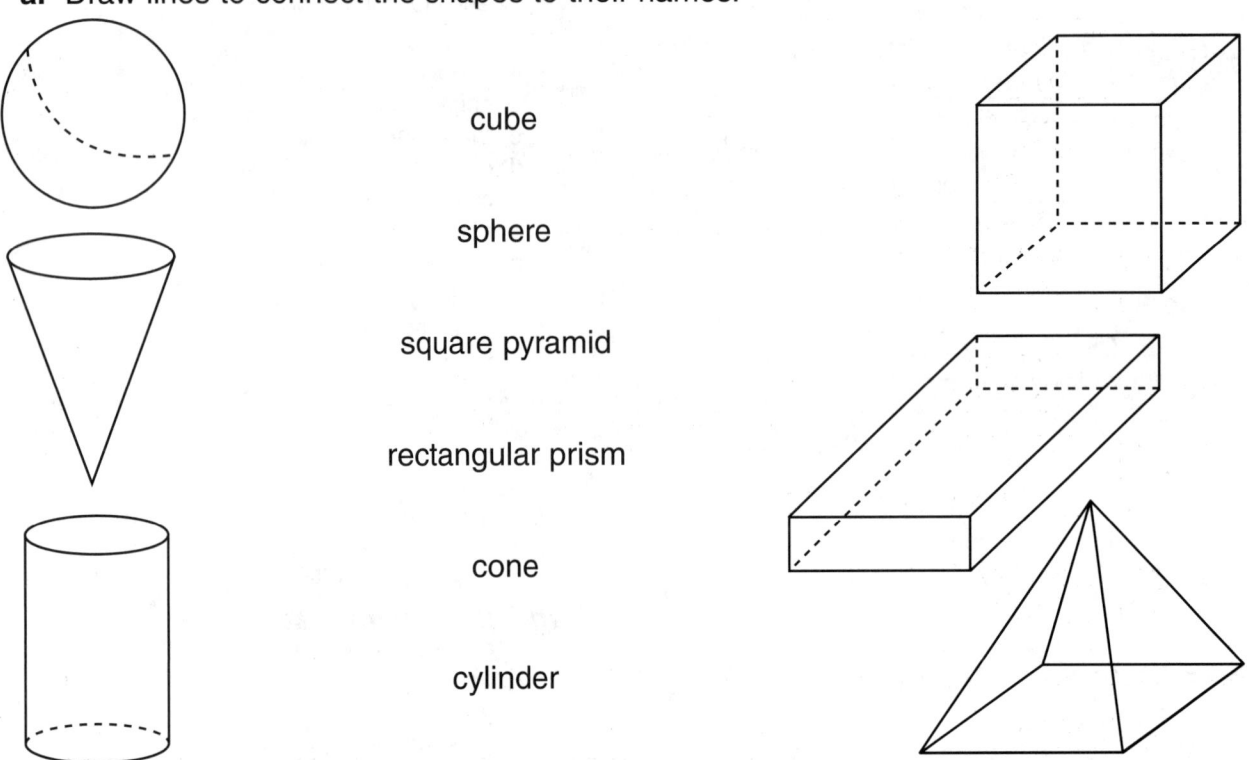

   cube

   sphere

   square pyramid

   rectangular prism

   cone

   cylinder

   b. Color the three-dimensional objects that have a curved surface red.

   c. Color the three-dimensional objects that have only flat surfaces blue.

2. Connect the dots to make these three objects.

   a.   b.   c.

       cube   triangular prism   square pyramid

3. Find five objects around the classroom that are the same shape as a cube. Write the names of these objects below.

   a. _____   b. _____

   c. _____   d. _____

   e. _____

#8995 Targeting Math: Geometry, Chance and Data   © Teacher Created Resources, Inc.

Three-Dimensional Shapes   *Pyramids*

Name **Date**

1. Match the label to the correct pyramid by coloring them in the same color.

   a.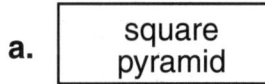
   b.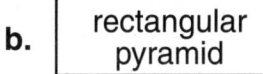
   c.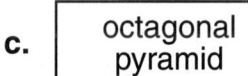
   d.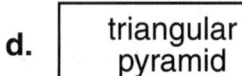
   e.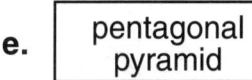
   f.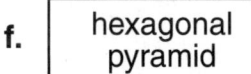

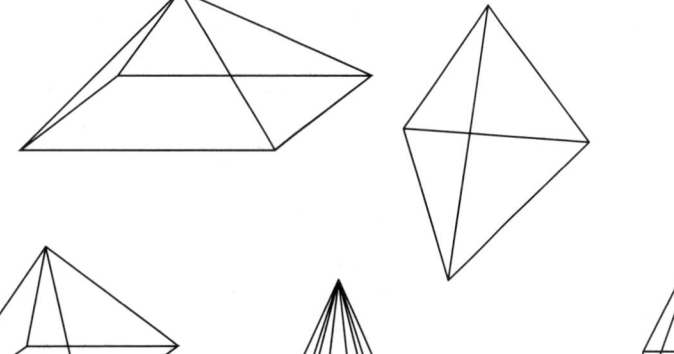

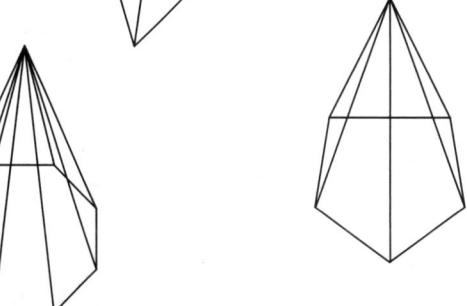

2. a. Draw a square pyramid and label one face, one corner, one edge, its base, and its apex.

   b. Draw all the faces of a square pyramid. One of the faces has already been drawn.

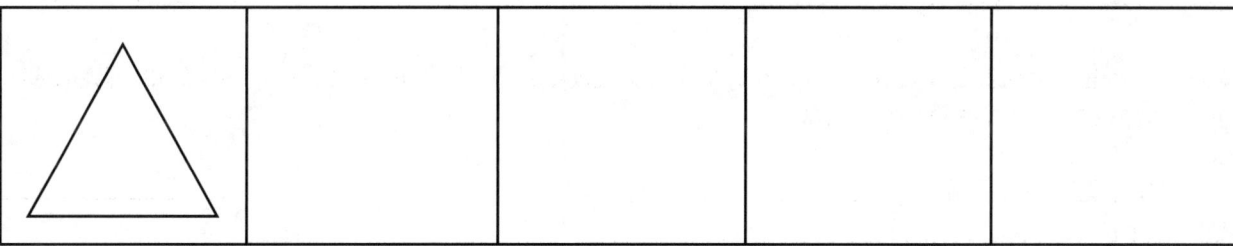

Three-Dimensional Shapes   Naming Geometric Solids

Name   **Date**

1. Name each of these objects.

   a. 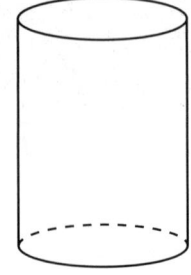   b. 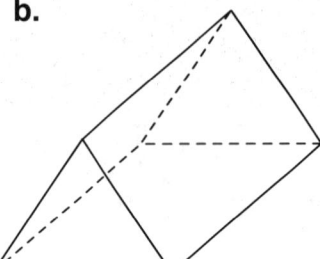   c. 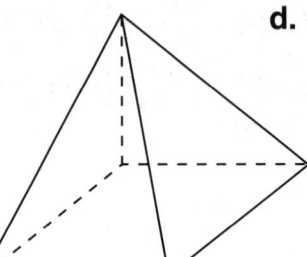   d.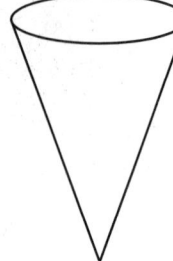

   _____   _____   _____   _____

   e. 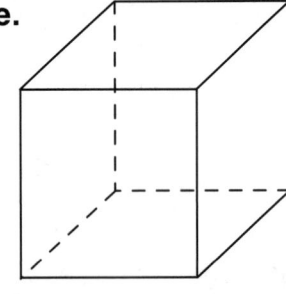   f. 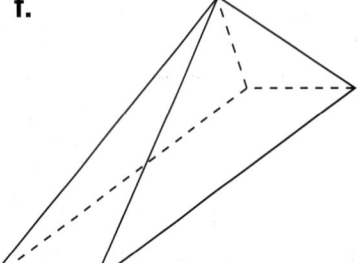   g.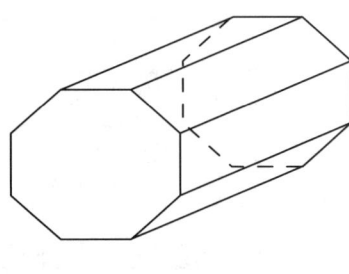

   _____   _____   _____

   h. Color the prisms red.
   i. Circle the pyramids.

2. a. Draw a prism. Name it. Color the base and label the faces (F), edges (E) and corners (C).

   b. Draw a pyramid. Name it. Color the base and label the faces (F), edges (E), corners, (C) and apex (A).

30

#8995 Targeting Math: Geometry, Chance and Data   © Teacher Created Resources, Inc.

Three-Dimensional Shapes Three-Dimensional Chart

Name **Date**

1. Complete the chart.

	Shape	Name	Number of Faces	Number of Edges	Number of Corners
a.					
b.					
c.					
d.					
e.					
f.					
g.					
h.					

© Teacher Created Resources, Inc. #8995 *Targeting Math: Geometry, Chance and Data*

Three-Dimensional Shapes   Cross-Sections

Name   **Date**

1. Draw the cross-section you would see if each of these objects was cut along the dashed line.

   a.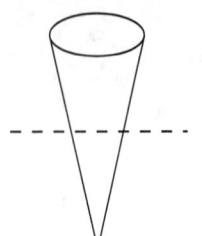

   b.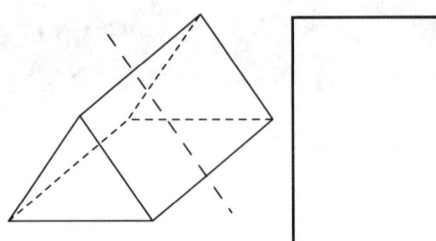

   c.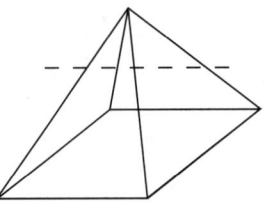

   d.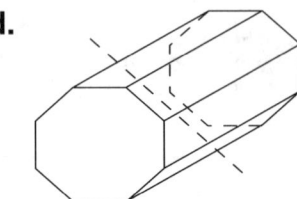

   e.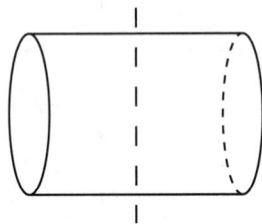

   f.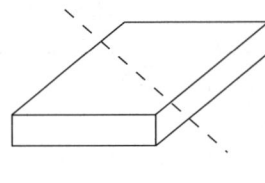

2. Draw a three-dimensional object from these shapes. Label the object that you have drawn.

   a.

   b.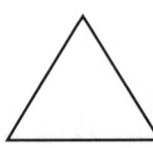

   _____   _____

   c.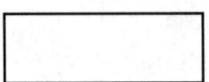

   d.

   _____   _____

#8995 Targeting Math: Geometry, Chance and Data   © Teacher Created Resources, Inc.

Three-Dimensional Shapes   Three-Dimensional Objects

Name   **Date**

1. a. Color the semi-spheres red.

   b. Color the rectangular prisms blue.

   c. Color the cylinders green.

   d. Color the cones yellow.

2. On the back of this page, draw six more three-dimensional objects to add to the picture. Write their names below.

   a. _____   b. _____

   c. _____   d. _____

33

© Teacher Created Resources, Inc.   #8995 Targeting Math: Geometry, Chance and Data

Three-Dimensional Shapes   Assessment

| **Name** | **Date** |

1. Name these three-dimensional objects.

   a. 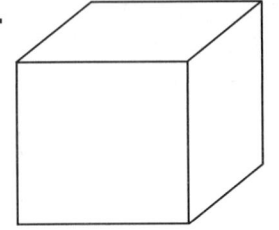   b. 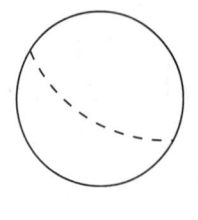   c. 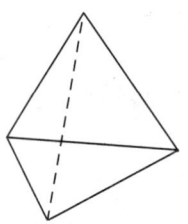   d.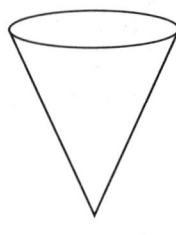

   _____   _____   _____   _____

   e. 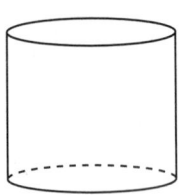   f. 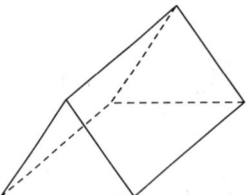   g. 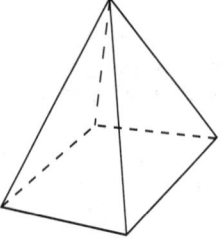   h.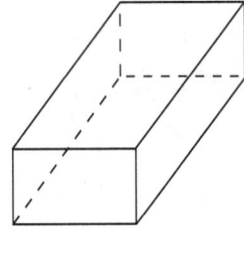

   _____   _____   _____   _____

2. Color the objects that are prisms.

3. Fill in the chart.

	Shape	Number of Faces	Number of Edges	Number of Corners
a.				
b.				
c.				

	Shape	Number of Faces	Number of Edges	Number of Corners
d.				
e.				
f.				

4. Draw the cross-sections of these three-dimensional objects.

   a. 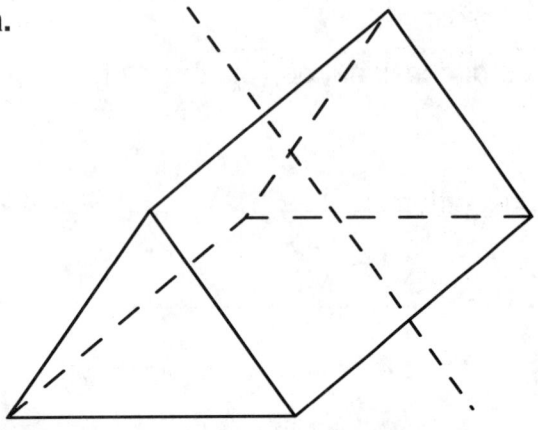   b.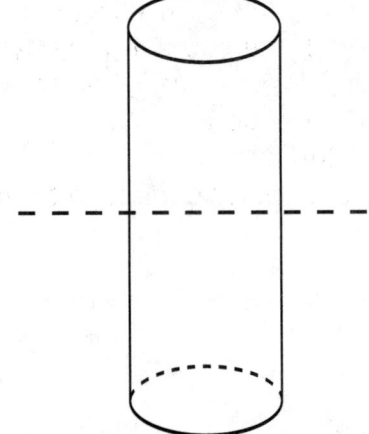

34

#8995 Targeting Math: Geometry, Chance and Data   © Teacher Created Resources, Inc.

Three-Dimensional Shapes   Activity Page

Name   **Date**

1. David and Joanna had to construct a large cube. It had to be 6 blocks long, 6 blocks high and 6 blocks wide.

   David has already built this.   Joanna has built this.

   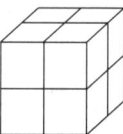

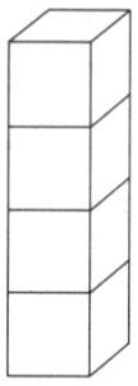

   a. How many cubes have both of them used so far?   _____

   b. How many cubes are needed altogether?   _____

   c. If they put their models together, how many more blocks will they need to make the larger cube?   _____

   d. Draw the large cube.

2. Simon has written some instructions to create a model. Try his instructions to make your own model.
   - I put a cube on the table.
   - Under the cube I placed a cylinder.
   - On top of the cube I placed a triangular pyramid.
   - Between the cube and the cylinder I placed a rectangular prism.
   - Next to the cylinder I placed 2 spheres.
   - Build the model.
   - Draw the model.
   - Add one more instruction to make your model different.

35

© Teacher Created Resources, Inc.   #8995 Targeting Math: Geometry, Chance and Data

THREE-DIMENSIONAL SHAPES

Unit 2
Drawing
Prisms
Cross-Sections
Views
Unfolded Figures

Objectives
- draw cross-sections of three-dimensional shapes
- match different prisms and pyramids with their unfolded figures
- discuss what is seen and not seen of an object from different positions and represent what is not seen
- identify and describe prisms and pyramids
- describe and compare the spatial features of mathematical objects
- identify, compare, classify, and construct three-dimensional objects and represent them in drawings

Language
edge, face, corner, flat, surface, curved, base, apex, cube, prism, pyramid, cylinder, cone, sphere, triangular, rectangular, cross-section, pentagonal, hexagonal, front, side, top

Materials/Resources
ruler, blank paper, colored pencils, three-dimensional objects made from wood (optional but very helpful)

Contents of Student Pages
* materials needed for each reproducible student page

Page 38 Drawing Objects
drawing and labeling; identifying objects

Page 39 Prisms
distinguishing between prisms and pyramids; faces, edges, corners, and apex

Page 40 Cross-Sections
drawing cross-sections; drawing different views
* colored pencils

Page 41 Completing Three-Dimensional Drawings
naming; creating a picture using three-dimensional objects

Page 42 Bases
looking at bases; prism patterns

Page 43 Views
top; side; front; three-dimensional objects; three-dimensional figures unfolded

Page 44 Assessment

Remember
Before starting, ensure that each student:
- ❑ develops the habit of checking all answers
- ❑ uses a ruler when drawing three-dimensional objects

#8995 Targeting Math: Geometry, Chance and Data © Teacher Created Resources, Inc.

Additional Activities
- Have students make three-dimensional objects from paper or cardboard. These make excellent mobiles.
- Have students construct objects using building blocks.
- Construct a class castle using only shapes made from prepared nets.
- Have students make a gift box or cylinder for Mother's Day, Father's Day, Christmas, etc.

Answers

Page 38 Naming Objects
1. Check individual answers.
2. a. triangular prism
   b. cylinder
   c. cone
   d. square pyramid
   e. cube
   f. rectangular prism
   g. triangular pyramid
   h. hexagonal prism
   i. sphere

Page 39 Prisms
1. Check individual answers.
2. prisms: a, b, e, and f
   pyramids: c and d
3. Check individual answers.

Page 40 Cross-Sections
1. Check individual answers.
2. Check individual answers.
3. Check individual answers.

Page 41 Completing Three-Dimensional Drawings
1. a. cylinder
   b. triangular prism
   c. triangular pyramid
   d. rectangular prism
   e. hexagonal pyramid
   f. cone
2. Check individual answers.

Page 42 Bases
1. a. triangular prism
   b. square prism
   c. cylinder
   d. octagonal prism
   e. pentagonal prism
   f. hexagonal prism
   g. decagonal prism
   h. septagonal prism
   i. rectangular prism
2. Check individual work.

Page 43 Views
1. Check individual answers.
2. a. cube
   b. pentagonal prism
   c. cylinder
   d. rectangular prism
   e. triangular prism

Page 44 Assessment
1. a. square pyramid
   b. cylinder
   c. pentagonal prism
   d. cone
   e. triangular pyramid
   f. sphere
   g. cube
   h. rectangular prism
2. Check individual answers.
3. Check individual answers.
4. Check individual answers.

© Teacher Created Resources, Inc. #8995 Targeting Math: Geometry, Chance and Data

Three-Dimensional Shapes | *Naming Objects*

| **Name** | **Date** |

1. Connect the dots to make these three objects.

a. 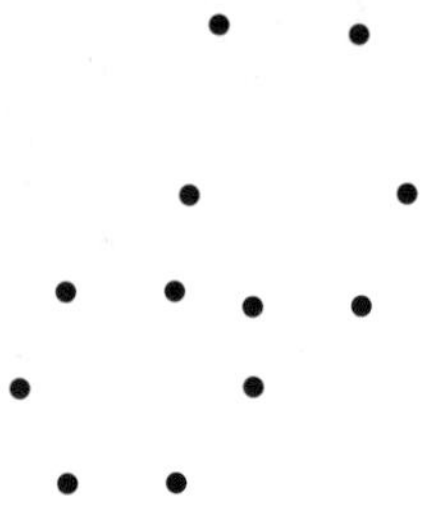
hexagonal prism

b.
triangular pyramid

c. 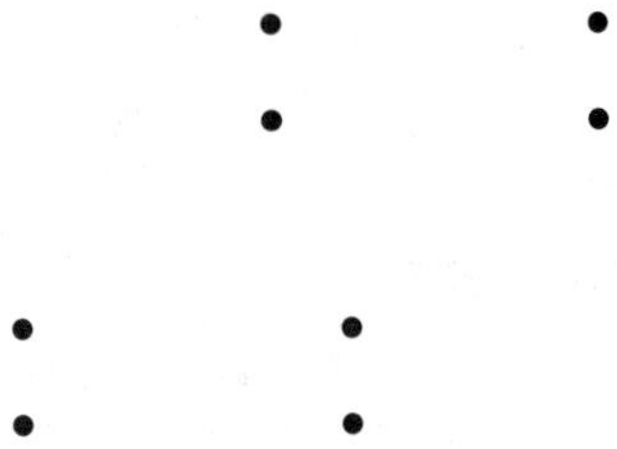
rectangular prism

2. Use the labels to name the following three-dimensional objects.
triangular prism, cube, sphere, cylinder, cone, square pyramid, rectangular prism, hexagonal prism, and triangular pyramid.

a. _____

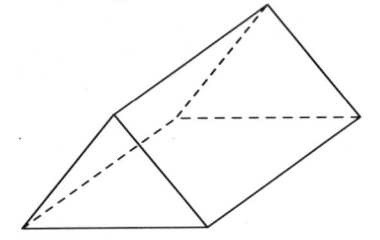

b. _____

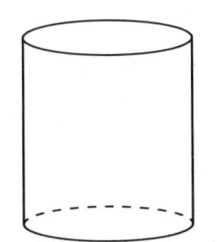

c. _____

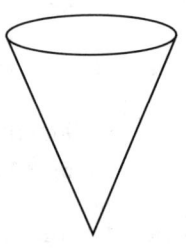

d. _____

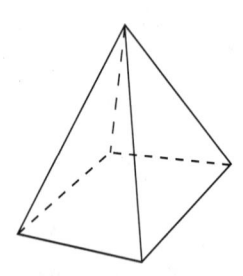

e. _____

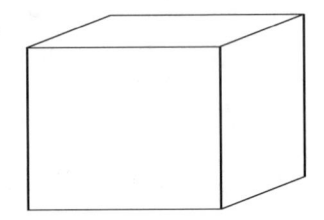

f. _____

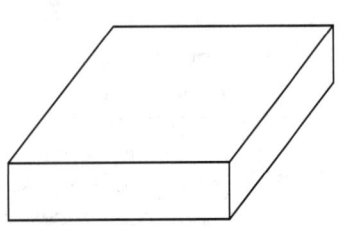

g. _____

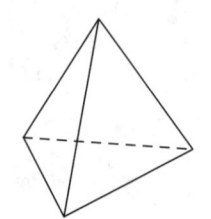

h. _____

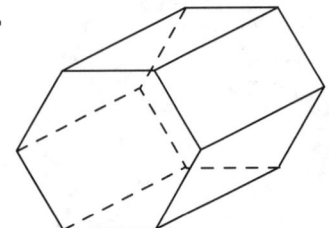

i. _____

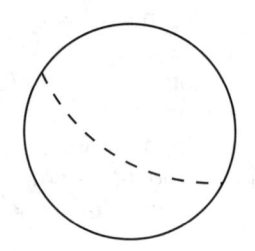

#8995 Targeting Math: Geometry, Chance and Data © Teacher Created Resources, Inc.

Three-Dimensional Shapes   Prisms

Name   **Date**

1. Draw three different prisms using the bases below.

   a.   b.   c.

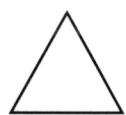

2. Circle the prisms and color the pyramids.

   a.   b. 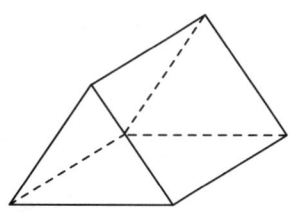   c.

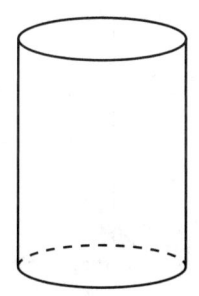

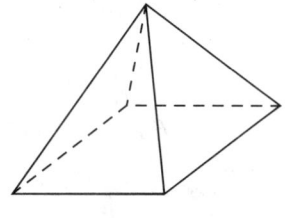

   d. 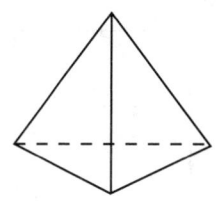   e. 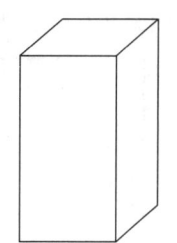   f.

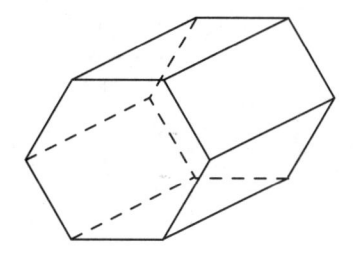

3. Label a face, an edge, and a corner on each three-dimensional object.

   a.   b.

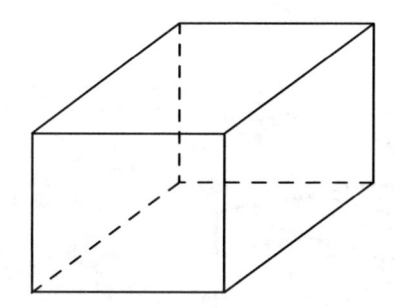

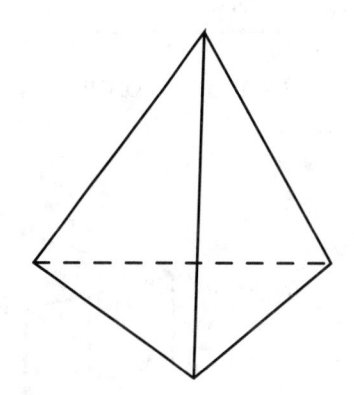

© Teacher Created Resources, Inc.   #8995 Targeting Math: Geometry, Chance and Data

Three-Dimensional Shapes　　　　　　　　　　　　　　　　　　　　　　*Cross-Sections*

Name　　　　　　　　　　　　　　　　　　**Date**

1. Draw the cross-section that you see when the object is cut along the dotted line.

   a.

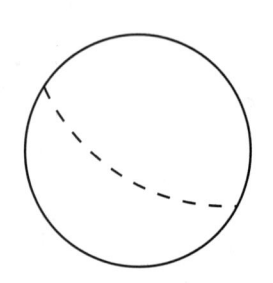

   b.

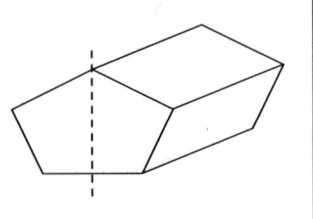

   c.

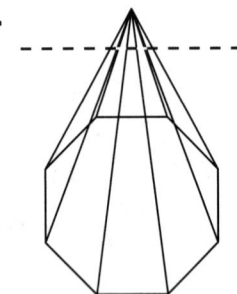

   d.

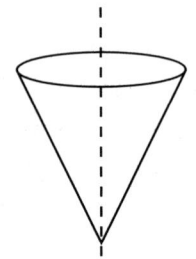

2. Choose an object in the room. Draw it from the front, side and top.

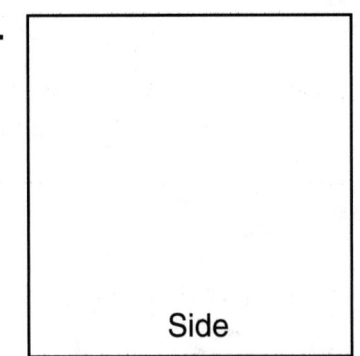

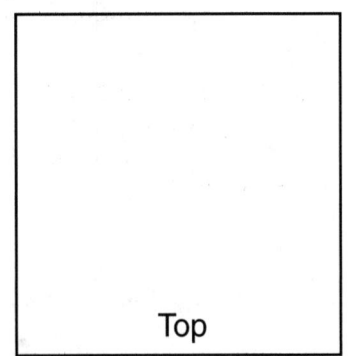

   a. Front

   b. Side

   c. Top

3. Make this present as colorful as you can.

#8995 Targeting Math: Geometry, Chance and Data　　　　　© Teacher Created Resources, Inc.

Three-Dimensional Shapes Completing Three-Dimensional Drawings

Name **Date**

1. Complete these three-dimensional objects and name them.

   a.   b.   c.

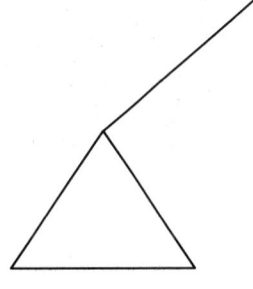

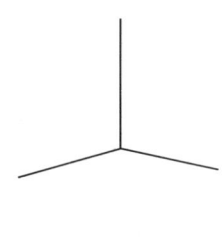

   _____   _____   _____

   d.   e.   f.

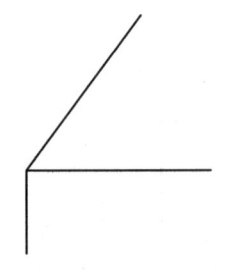

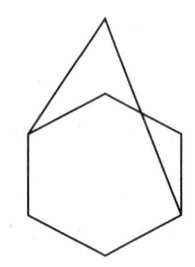

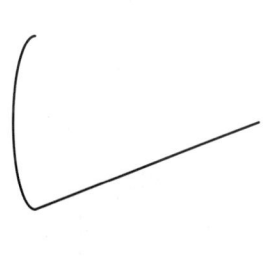

   _____   _____   _____

2. Create a picture using the following three-dimensional objects: cones, cylinders, triangular prisms, cubes, rectangular pyramids, and spheres.

Three-Dimensional Shapes   Bases

Name   **Date**

1. Label each of these prisms, then color the base of each prism.

   a. 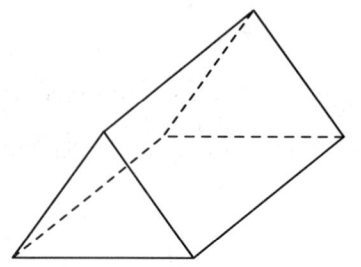   b. 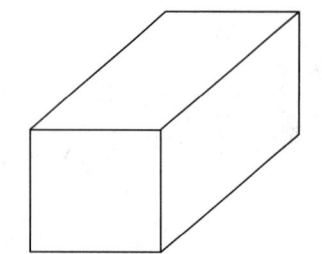   c.

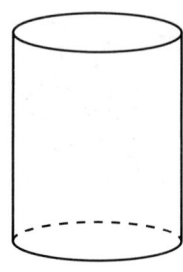

   _____   _____   _____
   d. 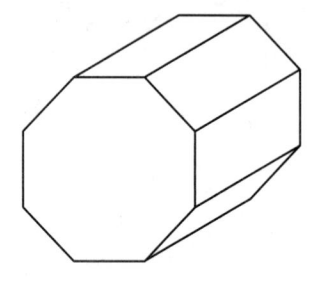   e. 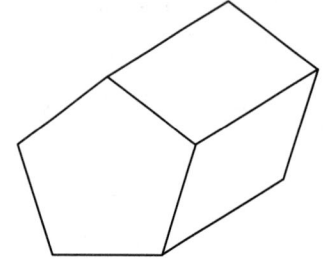   f.

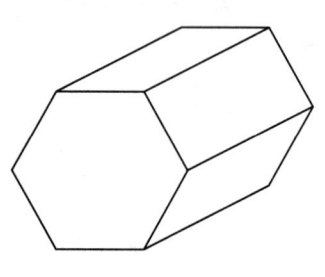

   _____   _____   _____
   g. 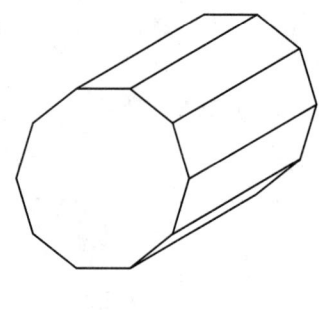   h. 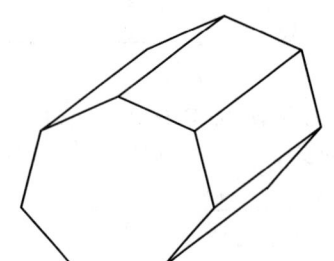   i.

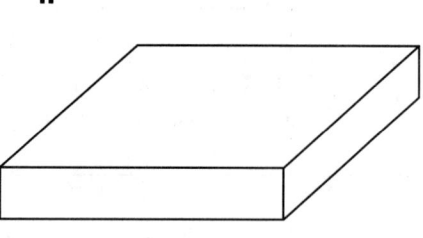

   _____   _____   _____

2. Complete these prism patterns.

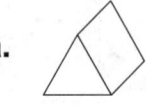

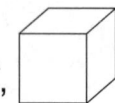

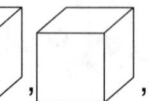

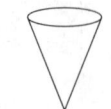

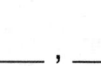

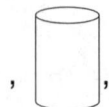

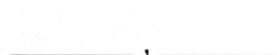

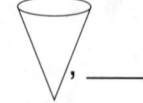

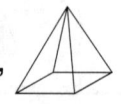

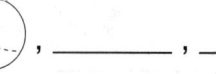

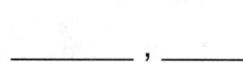

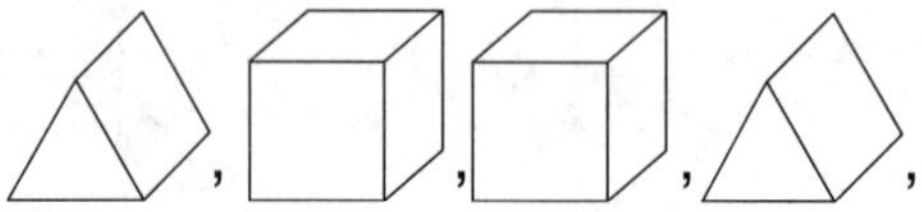

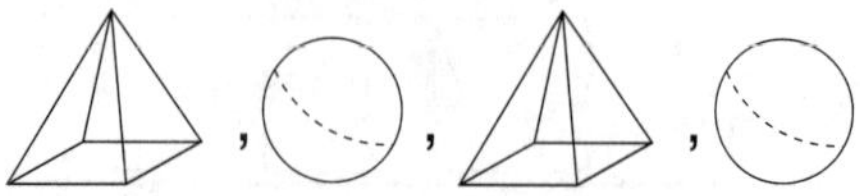

   a. △, ▢, ▢, △, _____, _____, _____, _____

   b. ▽, ▯, ▽, _____, _____, _____, _____, _____

   c. △, ○, △, ○, _____, _____, _____, _____

42

#8995 Targeting Math: Geometry, Chance and Data   © Teacher Created Resources, Inc.

Three-Dimensional Shapes *Views*

Name **Date**

1. Draw the front view, top view, and side view of each of these three-dimensional objects.

	Three-Dimensional Object	Top View	Front View	Side View
a.	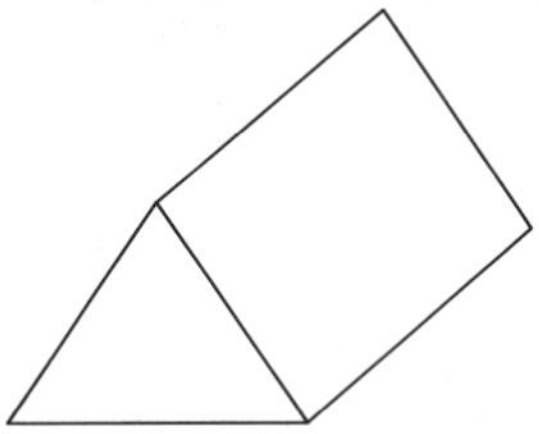			
b.	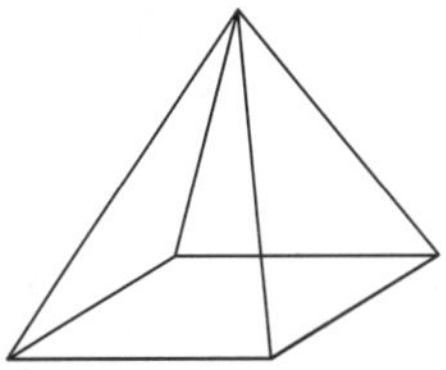			
c.	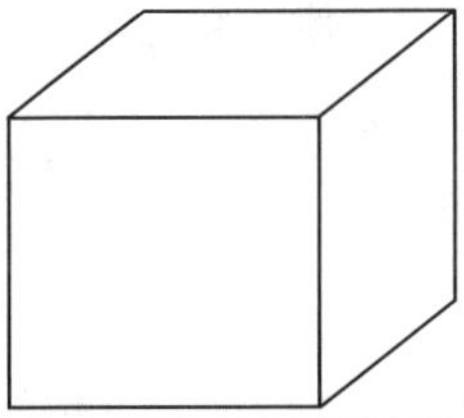			
d.	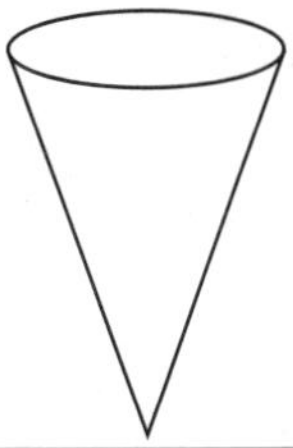			

2. Match the three-dimensional shapes to the correct unfolded figures.

a.

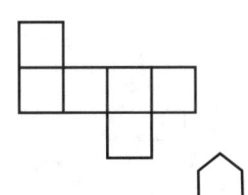

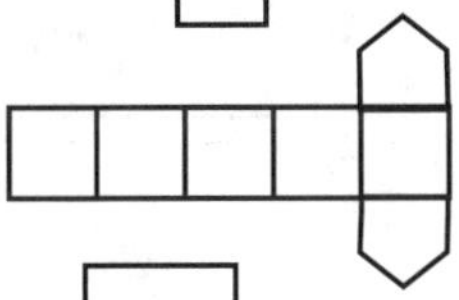

b.

c.

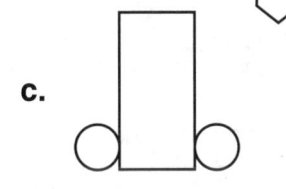

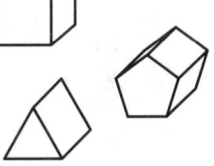

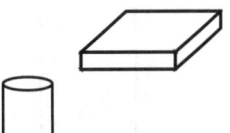

d.

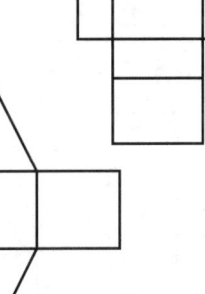

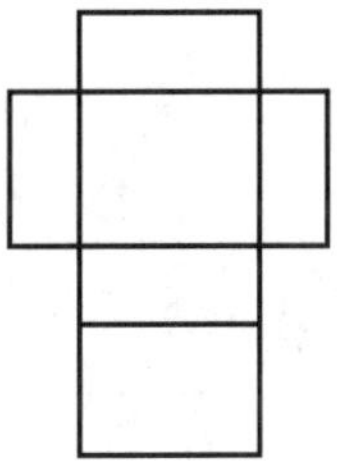

e.

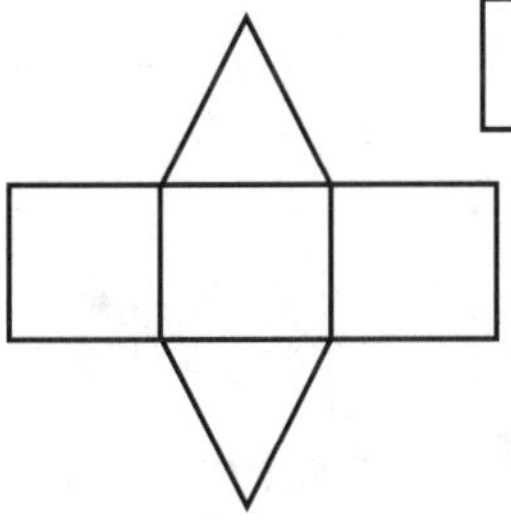

© Teacher Created Resources, Inc. #8995 *Targeting Math: Geometry, Chance and Data*

Three-Dimensional Shapes **Assessment**

| **Name** | **Date** |

1. Draw a line to match the names with the three-dimensional objects.

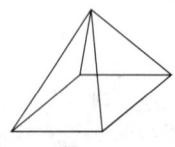

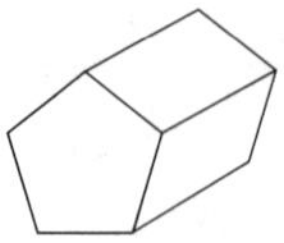

   a.   　　　　　　　　　cube　　　　　　　　e.

   　　　　　　　　　　　sphere

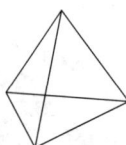

   b.　　　　　　　　square pyramid　　　　　f.

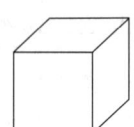

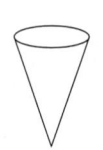

   　　　　　　　　rectangular prism

   　　　　　　　　triangular prism
   c.　　　　　　　　　　　　　　　　　　　　g.
   　　　　　　　　　　cylinder

   　　　　　　　　　　　cone
   d.　　　　　　　　　　　　　　　　　　　　h.
   　　　　　　　　pentagonal prism

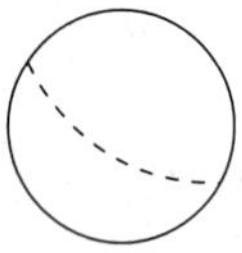

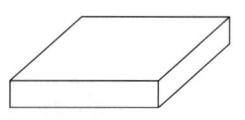

2. Label a face (F), an edge (E), a corner (C), and the apex (A) on these three-dimensional objects.

   a.　　　　　　　　　　　　　　　　b.

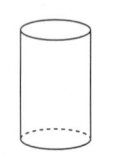

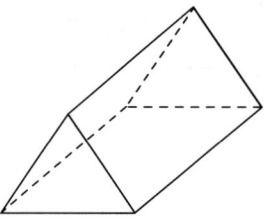

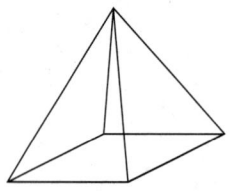

3. Draw the cross-section shown when the object is cut along the dotted line.

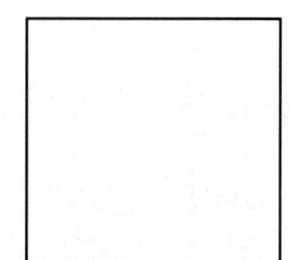

   a.　　　　　　　　　　　　　　　b.

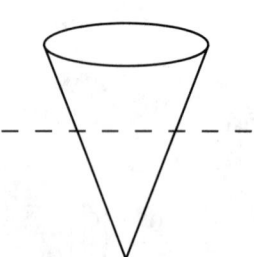

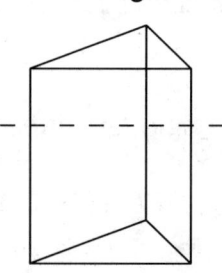

4. Draw:

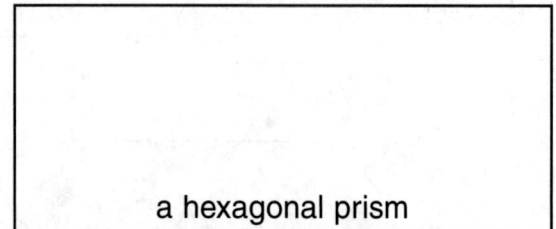

   a.　　　　　　　　　　　　　　　b.

   　　a hexagonal prism　　　　　　　　a pentagonal prism

44

#8995 Targeting Math: Geometry, Chance and Data　　　　　© Teacher Created Resources, Inc.

POSITION, MAPPING, TRANSFORMATION, AND SYMMETRY

The Position and Mapping unit uses the language of position on a number of exercises. Students follow directions, draw paths and maps, and use coordinates to locate specific items on grids. There are activities on drawing paths and finding coordinates. One assessment page is included.

The Transformation and Symmetry unit explores symmetry and making patterns through flipping, sliding, and turning. Tangram patterns are used to make pictures and lines of symmetry are drawn and counted. Two activity pages explore transformations and symmetry. One assessment page is included.

POSITION AND MAPPING

Unit 1

Directions
Maps
Coordinates
Dot-to-Dot
Position

Objectives
- use directional language in describing location
- note order and proximity on maps

Language
north, south, east, west, direction, instructions, position, map, coordinates, dot-to-dot, locating

Materials/Resources
pencils, rulers, colored pencils

Contents of Student Pages
* Materials needed for each reproducible student page

Page 48 Simple Directions
recognizing position and directions; following simple directions

Page 49 Following Directions
coloring a pathway; following directions to find position

Page 50 Reading Maps
giving directions from Point A to Point B; drawing maps
* colored pencils

Page 51 Position on Maps
locating position on maps, coordinate points

Page 52 Map Coordinates
locating position on maps; coordinate points

Page 53 Basic Geography
locating position on maps; understanding north, south, east, and west

Page 54 Assessment
* colored pencils

Page 55 Activity
drawing paths and solving a riddle

Remember

Before starting, ensure that each student:
- ❑ develops the habit of checking all answers.
- ❑ reads questions twice to avoid simple mistakes.
- ❑ knows the major compass points.

#8995 Targeting Math: Geometry, Chance and Data   © Teacher Created Resources, Inc.

Additional Activities

❑ Have students use a street directory to find their cities and home addresses. Using the street directory, they can follow the streets to their school.

❑ Have students write directions from their desks in the classroom to a secret location (e.g., 3 steps forward, 10 steps to the right). They then give the instructions to a friend to see if the friend will end up at the secret location.

❑ Help students collect different maps to show that there are many ways of mapping locations (e.g., navigation, sailing maps, road maps, house plans, etc.).

❑ Have students draw maps of their houses and concentrate on floor plans.

Answers

Page 48 Simple Directions
1. a. left
   b. in
   c. next to
   d. right
   e. beside
2. a. A
   b. G
   c. V
   d. L

Page 49 Following Directions
1. a. Check individual work.
   b. three down, one right, two down, three right, two down, three right, two up, three right, three down
2. a. Tim
   b. Kate
   c. Greg
   d. Back row, right corner

Page 50 Reading Maps
Check individual work.

Page 51 Position on Maps
1. a. C4
   b. E3
   c. B3
   d. G5
   e. G2
   f. G4
2. a. Mount Isle
   b. Pitt Town
   c. Emu Wharf
   d. Point Change
   e. Street Beach
   f. Freeway Ocean

Page 52 Map Coordinates
1. a. Glenmore Valley
   b. Pine Point
   c. Blue Mountain
   d. Forest Way
   e. Logan Lookout
   f. Wing Point
2. a. B4
   b. G3
   c. D6
   d. F5
   e. F6
   f. D2
3. a. Timmins
   b. west
   c. east
   d. northwest

Page 53 Basic Geography
1. Answers will vary.
2. Atlantic Ocean and Indian Ocean
3. Indian Ocean
4. North America and South America
5. Atlantic Ocean
6. South America

Page 54 Assessment
1. a. F
   b. J
   c. T
   d. H
2. 3 right, 2 down, 2 right, 2 up, 3 right, 3 down, 2 right
3. a. C2
   b. D5
   c. I2
   d. B3
4. Check individual work.

Page 55 Activity
1. Check individual work.
2. "Man, have I got problems."

© Teacher Created Resources, Inc.

#8995 Targeting Math: Geometry, Chance and Data

Position and Mapping | Simple Directions

Name | **Date**

1. Circle the correct word in each sentence so that it relates to the picture.

   a. The hut is on the left/right side of the creek.

   b. The fish are in/beside the creek.

   c. The hut is next to/far away from the creek.

   d. The tree is on the right/left side of the creek.

   e. The girl is standing on top of/beside the hut.

2. Follow the directions to find the letters.

A	B	C	D	E	F	G	H
I	J	K	L	M	N	O	P
Q	R	S	T	U	V	W	X
Y	Z	A	B	C	D	E	F

   a. The bottom row, third from the left. _____

   b. Top row, second from the right. _____

   c. Second row from the bottom, third from the right. _____

   d. Third row from the bottom, fourth from the left. _____

48

#8995 Targeting Math: Geometry, Chance and Data © Teacher Created Resources, Inc.

Position and Mapping　　　　　　　　　　　　　　　　　　　　　　　Following Directions

Name　　　　　　　　　　　　　　　　　　　　**Date**

1. **a.** Follow the directions and color your path from home to school.

   3 forward, 2 down, 4 right, 1 down, 2 left, 4 down, 6 right

   home

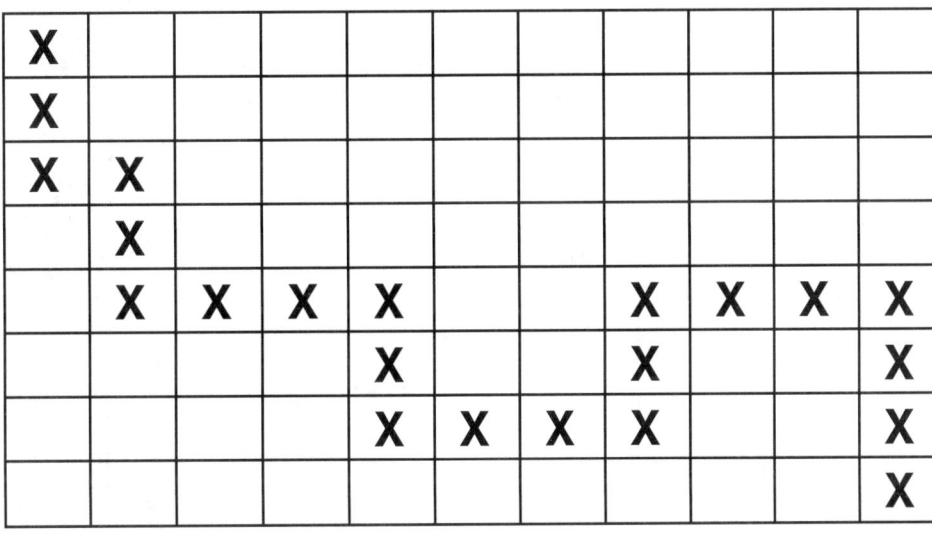

X									
X									
X	X								
	X								
	X	X	X	X		X	X	X	X
				X			X		X
				X	X	X	X		X
									X

   school

   b. Write the directions for the path that has been marked with an "X."

   _____

   _____

   _____

2. Look at the map of this classroom. Answer the following questions.

   Back

Tom	Kate	Dee	Scott	Bob
Lee	Kirst	Greg	Gillian	Joe
Steve	John	Tim	Betty	Jim

   　　　　　　　Teacher

   a. Who sits directly in front of the teacher? _____

   b. Who sits in the back row, second from the left? _____

   c. Who sits in the second row in the center? _____

   d. Write the position of Bob's seat. _____

© Teacher Created Resources, Inc.　　　　　　#8995 Targeting Math: Geometry, Chance and Data

Position and Mapping

Reading Maps

Name **Date**

1. Color two paths from home to the supermarket. Write the directions for the shorter path.

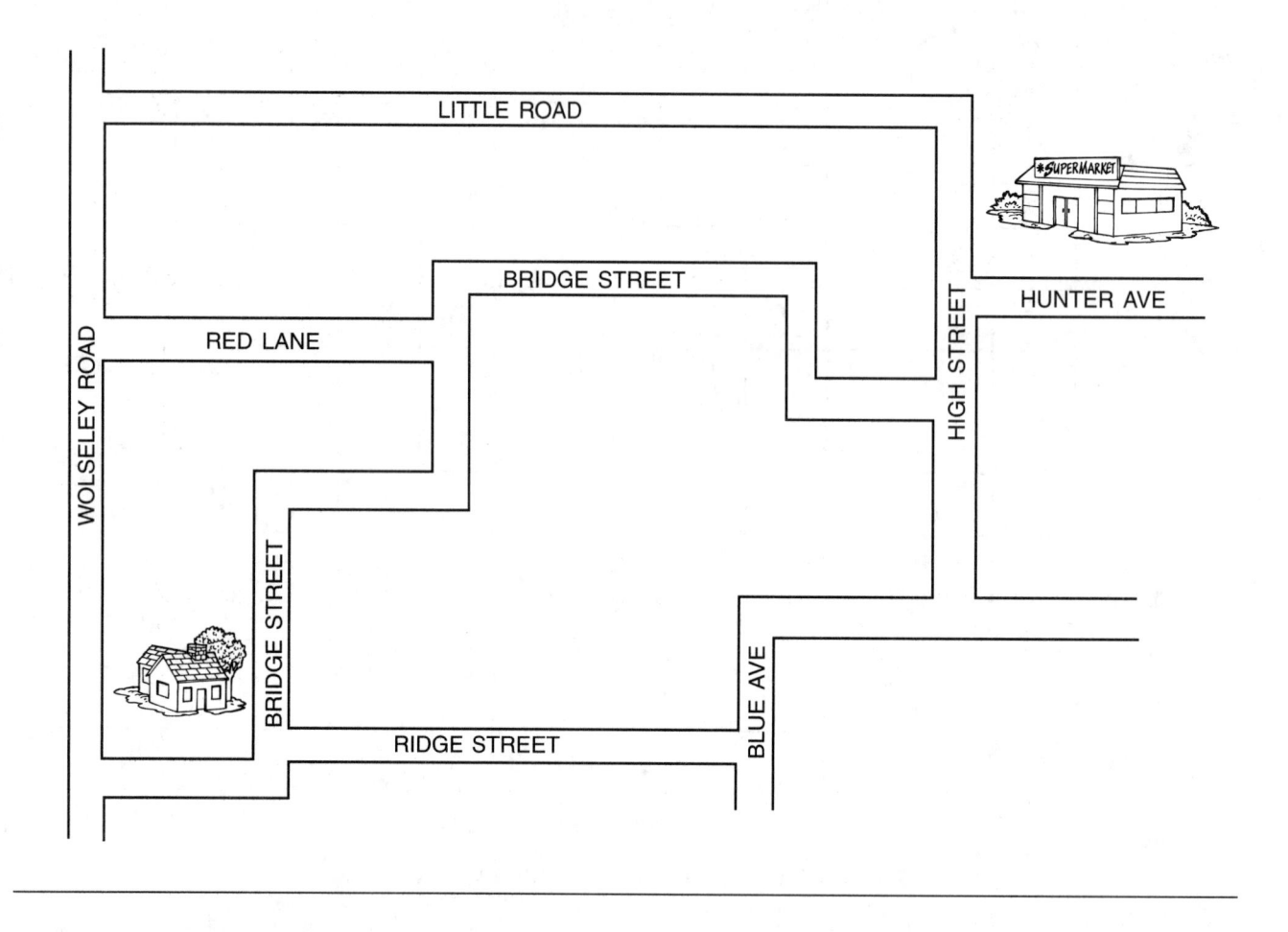

_____
_____
_____

2. Draw a map of how you get to school.

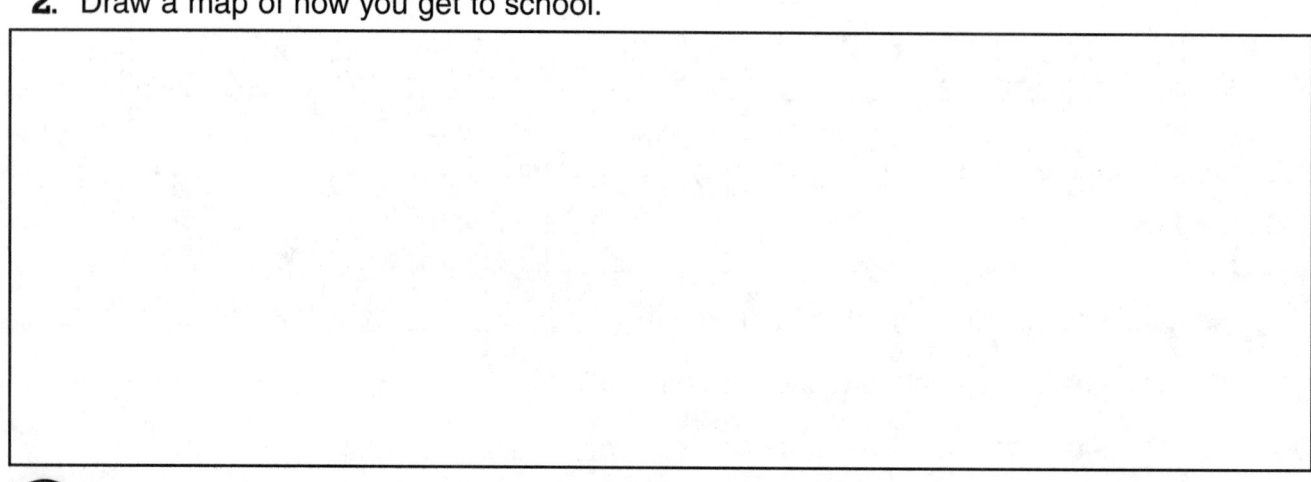

#8995 Targeting Math: Geometry, Chance and Data © Teacher Created Resources, Inc.

Position and Mapping *Position on Maps*

Name **Date**

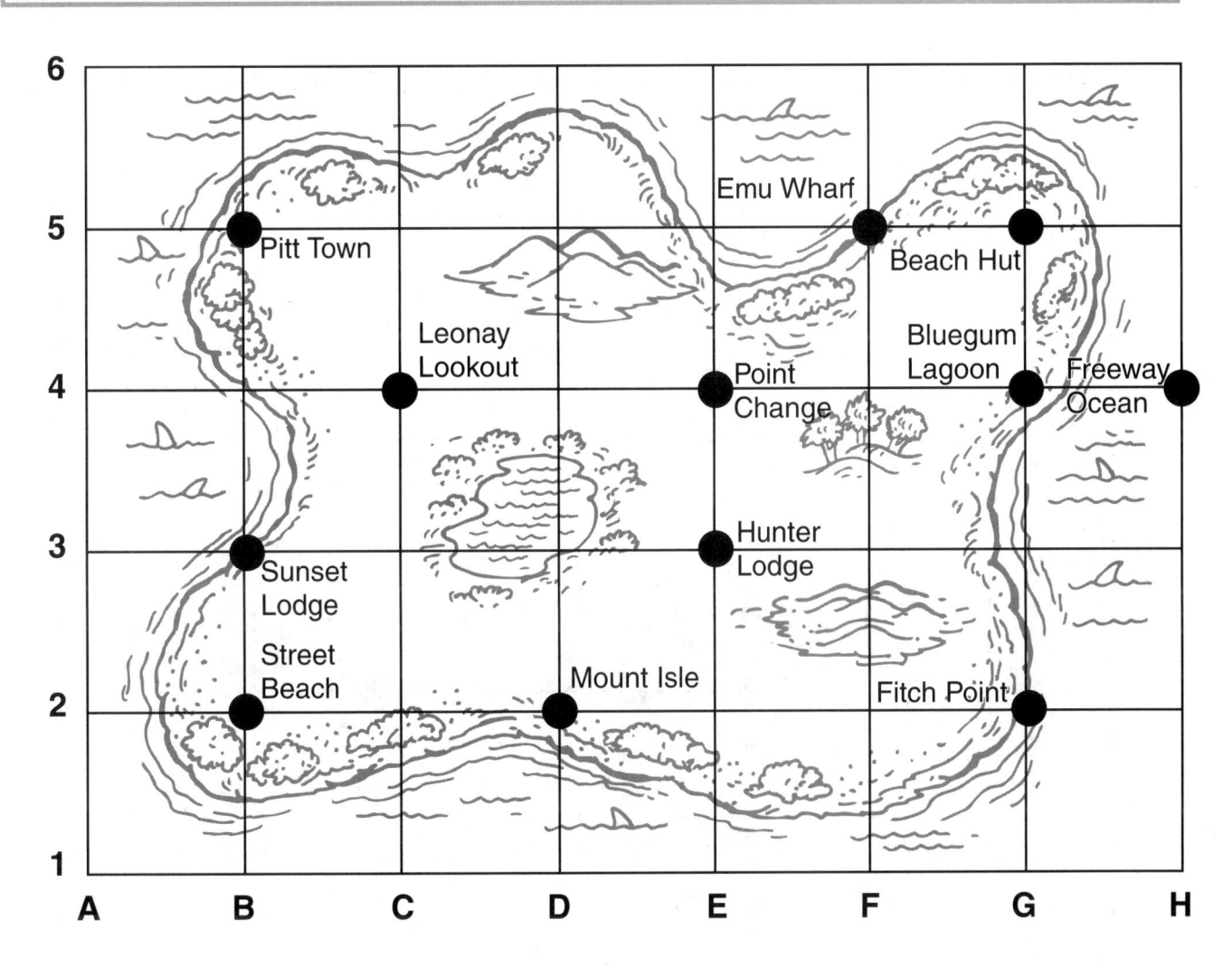

1. Give the position coordinates for the following locations on Emu Island.

   a. Leonay Lookout _____   b. Hunter Lodge _____

   c. Sunset Lodge _____   d. Beach Hut _____

   e. Fitch Point _____   f. Bluegum Lagoon _____

2. What is located at the following points?

   a. D2 _____   b. B5 _____

   c. F5 _____   d. E4 _____

   e. B2 _____   f. H4 _____

Position and Mapping　　　　　　　　　　　　　　　　　　　　　　Map Coordinates

Name　　　　　　　　　　　　　　**Date**

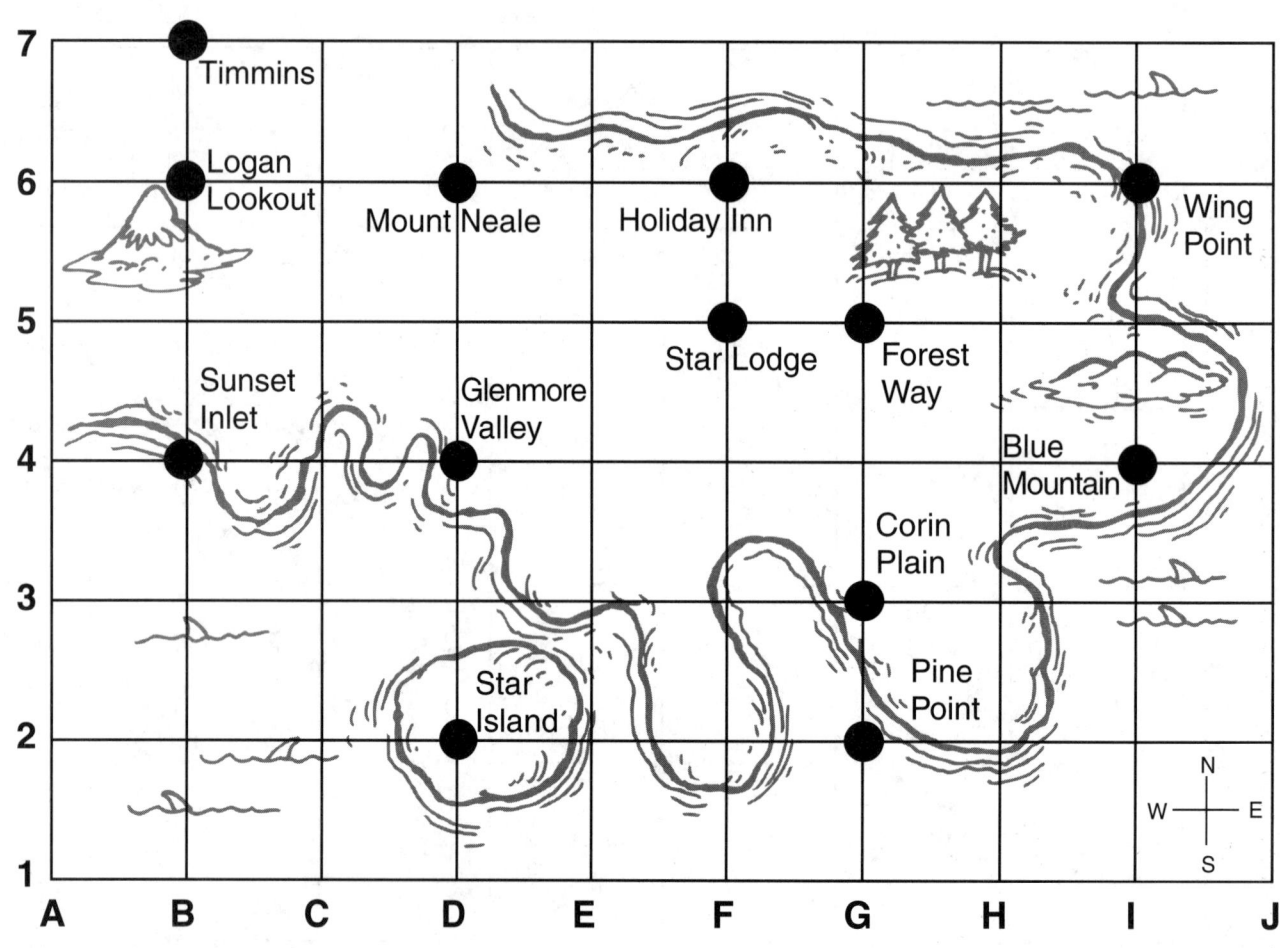

1. Name the places at these coordinates.

    a. D4 _____   b. G2 _____

    c. I4 _____   d. G5 _____

    e. B6 _____   f. I6 _____

2. Give the coordinates for the following places.

    a. Sunset Inlet _____   b. Corin Plain _____

    c. Mount Neale _____   d. Star Lodge _____

    e. Holiday Inn _____   f. Star Island _____

3. a. What is the most northerly town on the map? _____

    b. What direction is Star Island from Pine Point? _____

    c. What directions is Blue Mountain from Glenmore Valley? _____

    d. What direction is Logan Lookout from Forest Way? _____

Position and Mapping Basic Geography

Name **Date**

A world map is another kind of map that is often used. It shows oceans and land masses. There are four oceans and seven continents. Use the world map below to answer the questions.

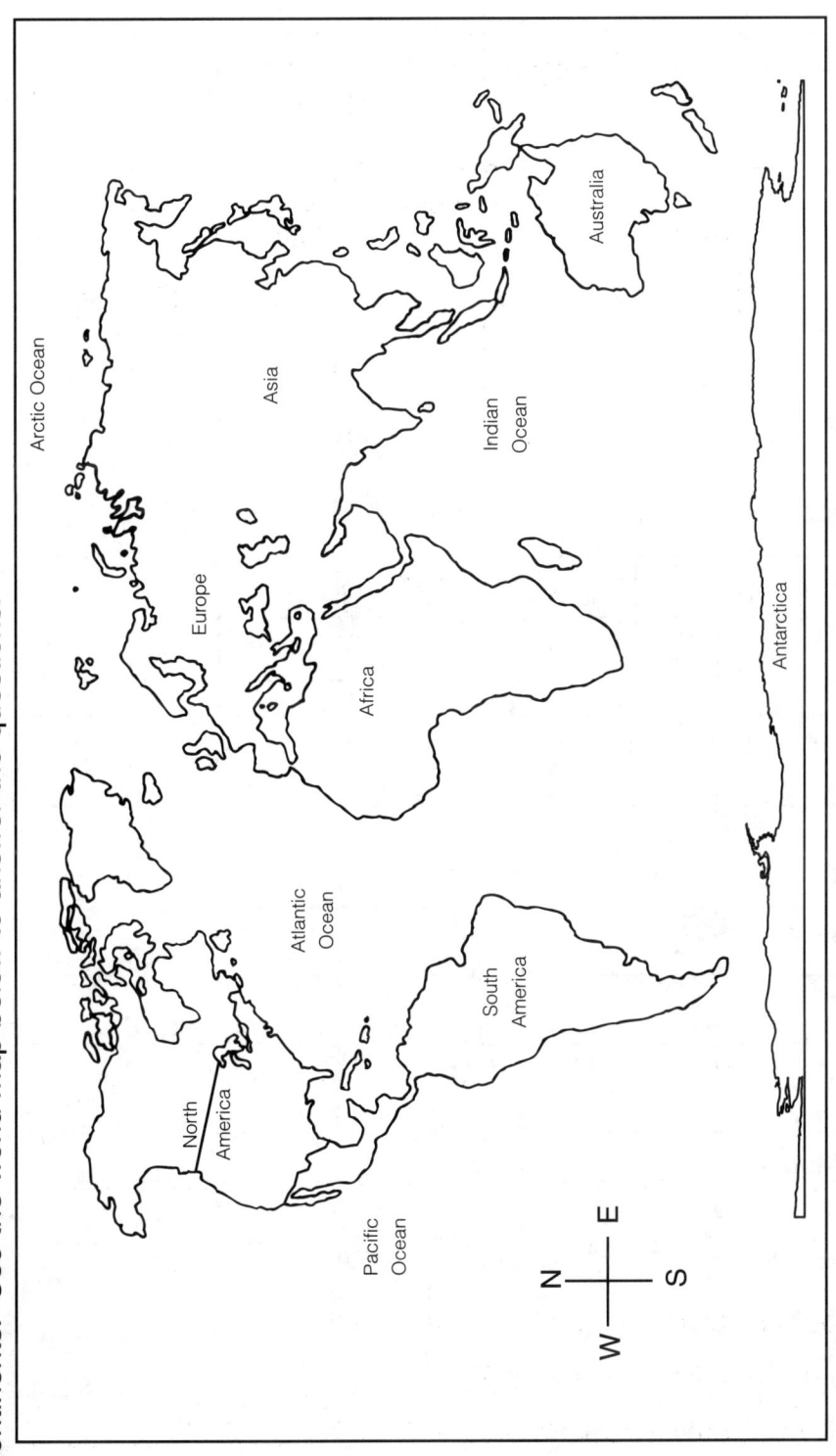

[World map showing continents labeled: North America, South America, Europe, Africa, Asia, Australia, Antarctica; and oceans labeled: Arctic Ocean, Atlantic Ocean, Pacific Ocean, Indian Ocean. Compass rose showing N, E, S, W.]

1. What is the name of the continent on which you live? _____
2. Which two oceans border Africa? _____
3. What ocean is south of Asia? _____
4. Which two continents are to the east of the Pacific Ocean? _____
5. Which ocean separates North America from Europe? _____
6. Which continent is closest to Antarctica? _____

© *Teacher Created Resources, Inc.* #8995 *Targeting Math: Geometry, Chance and Data*

53

Position and Mapping   Assessment

Name   **Date**

1. Which letter is found in the following positions?

a	b	c	d	e	f	g	h
i	j	k	l	m	n	o	p
q	r	s	t	u	v	w	x

   a. Top row, third from the right _____

   b. Second row, second from the left _____

   c. Bottom row, fifth from the right _____

   d. Top row, right corner _____

2. Use the back of this paper to write the directions for the path marked with an "X."

   Start →
X	X	X		X	X	X	X		
		X		X			X		
		X	X	X			X		
							X	X	X	Finish

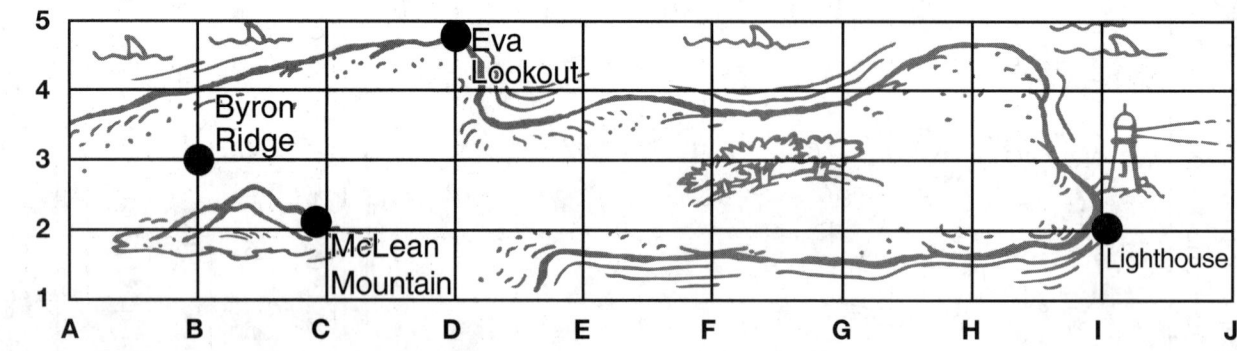

3. Map with coordinates A–J horizontal and 1–5 vertical. Locations shown: Byron Ridge, Eva Lookout, McLean Mountain, Lighthouse.

   Give the coordinates for the following locations on the map.

   a. McLean Mountain _____   b. Eva Lookout _____

   c. Lighthouse _____   d. Byron Ridge _____

4. Insert these locations on the map.

   a. E3, Small Town   b. G2, Turner Lake   c. H4, High Village

(54)

#8995 Targeting Math: Geometry, Chance and Data   © Teacher Created Resources, Inc.

Position and Mapping Activity Page

Name **Date**

1.

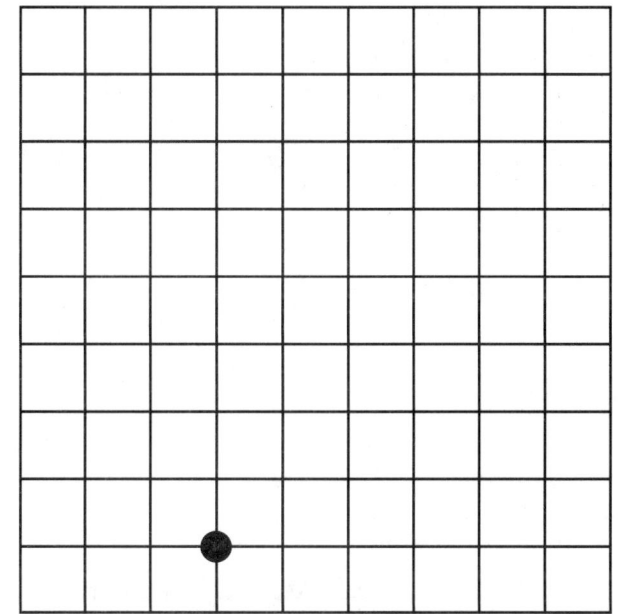

Start at the dot to draw this path.
Go up 7, right 4, down 1, left 3, down 2, right 2, down 1, left 2, down 2, right 3, down 1, left 4.

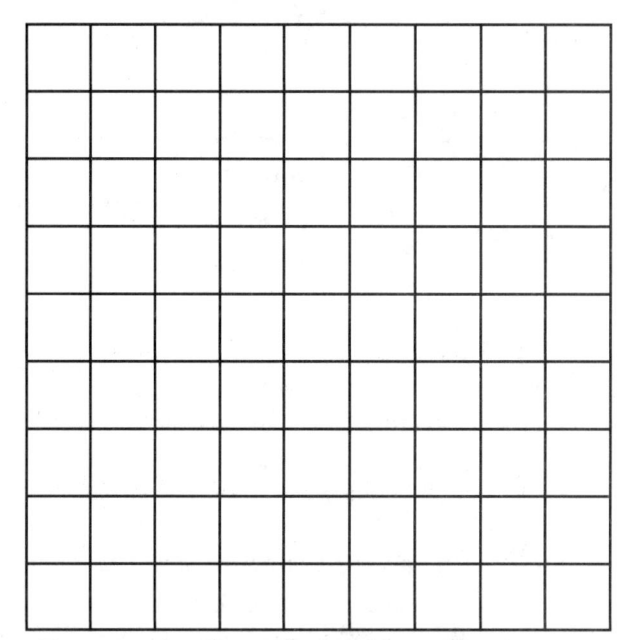

Draw a simple path on this grid. Describe it to a friend who will then try to draw it.

2. Complete the riddle below by matching the letters on the grid with the clues.

What did one math book say to the other?

	1	2	3	4	5	6	7	8	9	10	11	12	13	14
H	A	A	S	R	D	T	C	X	Q	W	I	W	I	I
G	R	F	B	E	V	Z	E	P	N	F	G	H	L	J
F	D	E	M	U	T	E	O	B	Z	H	U	V	J	W
E	U	E	D	A	K	O	J	X	I	O	Q	R	G	X
D	M	Y	B	X	O	G	A	H	P	J	K	S	D	K
C	H	L	L	Q	P	L	M	N	C	C	I	A	L	M
B	N	T	V	X	V	G	D	Z	S	H	Y	X	V	N
A	O	U	E	V	U	F	W	O	Q	Z	W	P	M	O

"__ __ __ , __ __ __ , __ __ __ __ __
(3, F) (7, D) (9, G) (1, C) (12, C) (3,B), (4, G) (11, H) (13, E) (10, E) (6, H)
"
__ __ __ __ __ __ __ __
(5, C) (1, G) (8, A) (3, D) (13, G) (6, F) (13, A) (9, B)

© Teacher Created Resources, Inc.   #8995 *Targeting Math: Geometry, Chance and Data*

TRANSFORMATION AND SYMMETRY

Unit 2

Flip
Slide
Turn
Symmetry
Patterns

Objectives

- describe patterns in terms of flips, slides, and turns; and create puzzles, tessellations and other patterns
- visualize and describe patterns in terms of flipping and sliding
- construct patterns using flips, slides, and turns
- construct and assemble tangram puzzles
- make and identify symmetrical patterns
- make and identify symmetrical shapes
- recognize symmetry in the environment

Language

flip, slide, turn, symmetry, patterns, tangram, puzzle, shapes, half, line

Materials/Resources

pencils, ruler, blank paper, scissors, a piece of colored cardboard, colored pencils

Contents of Student Pages

* Materials needed for each reproducible student page

Page 58 Flip, Slide, and Turn
completing a table; making a pattern

Page 59 Tangrams
making a tangram puzzle; creating puzzle pictures
* scissors
* colored cardstock
* blank paper (optional)

Page 60 Lines of Symmetry
drawing line of symmetry; lines in shapes; pictures
* colored pencils

Page 61 Symmetry
drawing and counting lines of symmetry; coloring symmetrical shapes
* colored pencils

Page 62 More Lines of Symmetry
drawing and counting lines of symmetry; completing a symmetrical picture

Page 63 Patterns
creating patterns using flip and slide.
* colored pencils

Page 64 Assessment

Page 65 Activity
making patterns through tessellation and reflection

Page 66 Activity
finding opposite patterns

Remember

Before starting ensure that each student:
❑ understands the importance of using a ruler to draw all lines.
❑ remembers to read all instructions before starting questions.

#8995 Targeting Math: Geometry, Chance and Data   © Teacher Created Resources, Inc.

Additional Activities

❑ Have students fold a sheet of paper in half and put some paint on the fold line. They can then pat the sides of the paper together, and open the paper fold to find a symmetrical painting.

❑ Have students make "enormous" tangram puzzle pieces to create floor puzzles.

❑ Students can cut out shapes and fold on lines of symmetry to visually understand the "line of symmetry."

❑ Create a class collage of student-created patterns.

❑ Have students look for and record examples of symmetry on the playground.

Answers

Page 58 Flip, Slide, and Turn

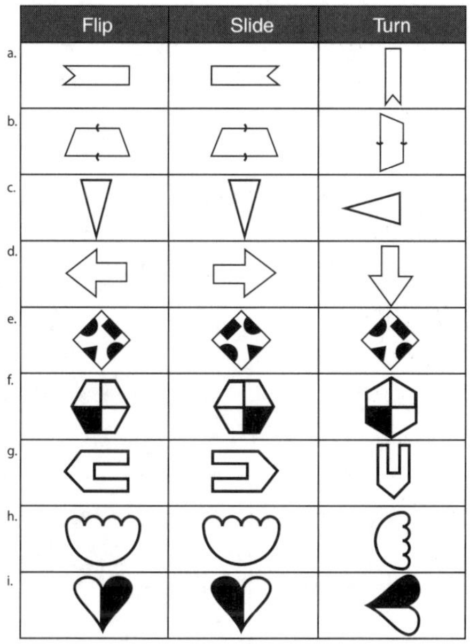

2. Check individual work.

Page 59 Tangrams
Check individual work.

Page 60 Lines of Symmetry
1. Check individual work.
2. a. 6   b. 2   c. 1   d. 4 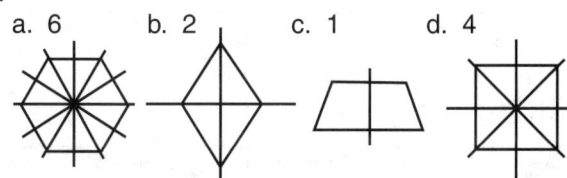
3. Check individual work.

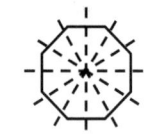

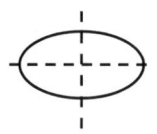

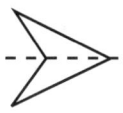

Page 61 Symmetry
1. a. 8   b. 1   c. 2   d. 1
2. Check individual work.
3. Color b, d, e, f, g, h

Page 62 More Lines of Symmetry
1. a. B   b. D   c. T   d. I   e. C
2. a. 2   b. 4   c. 1   d. 1
   e. 2   f. 3   g. 2   h. 8
3. Check individual work

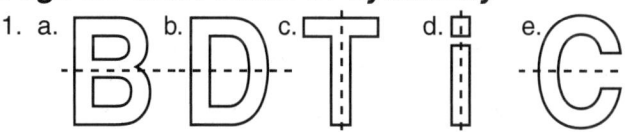

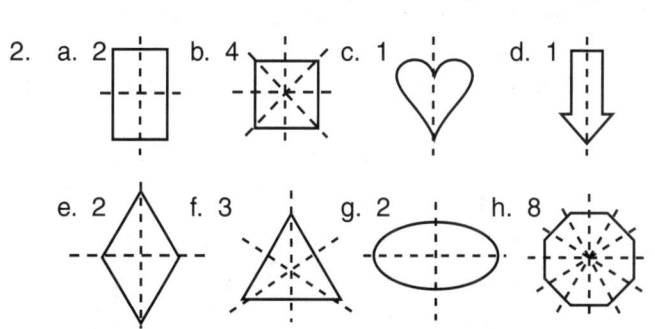

Page 63 Patterns
Check individual work.

Page 64 Assessment
1. a., b., c. 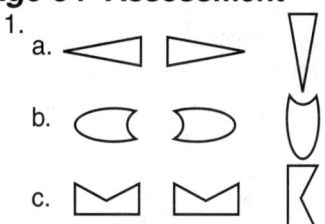
2. Check individual work.
3. a. 2   c. 1
   b. 6   d. 3
4. Check individual work.
5. Check individual work.

Page 65 Activity
Check individual work.

Page 66 Activity
1. c   4. b
2. c   5. d
3. b

© Teacher Created Resources, Inc.   #8995 Targeting Math: Geometry, Chance and Data

Transformation and Symmetry   *Flip, Slide, and Turn*

Name   **Date**

1. Complete the chart.

	Shape	Flip	Slide	Turn
a.				
b.				
c.				
d.				
e.				
f.				
g.				
h.				
i.				

2. Draw your own shape, then flip, slide, and turn it to make a pattern. Use the back of this page.

#8995 Targeting Math: Geometry, Chance and Data   © Teacher Created Resources, Inc.

Transformation and Symmetry — *Tangrams*

Name   **Date**

1. Copy this tangram onto colored cardstock. Cut out the seven pieces of this tangram.

2. Make three shapes using your tangram pieces. Draw your shapes on a blank piece of paper.

© Teacher Created Resources, Inc.   #8995 *Targeting Math: Geometry, Chance and Data*

Transformation and Symmetry   Lines of Symmetry

1. Draw **one** line of symmetry through each of these shapes and color half of the shape.
   a.   b. 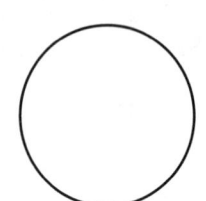   c. 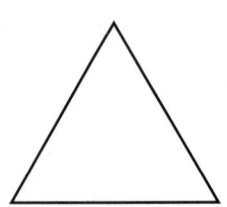   d.

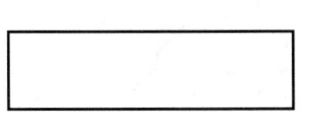

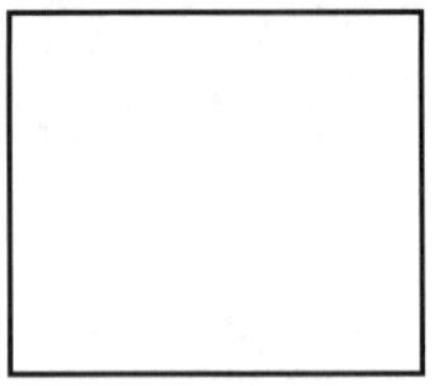

2. Draw **all** the lines of symmetry for each of these shapes and count them. Write the number you find on the line under the shape.
   a.   b.   c.   d.

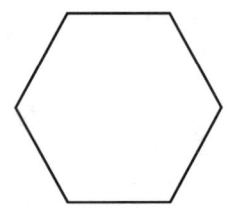

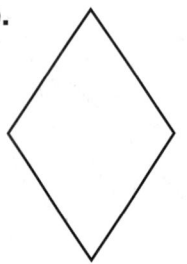

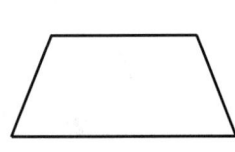

   _____   _____   _____   _____

3. Complete the other half of each picture on the line of symmetry.
   a.   b.

   c.    d.

60

#8995 Targeting Math: Geometry, Chance and Data   © Teacher Created Resources, Inc.

Transformation and Symmetry Symmetry

Name **Date**

1. Draw and count the lines of symmetry in these shapes.

   a. 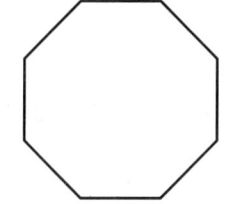 b.  c. 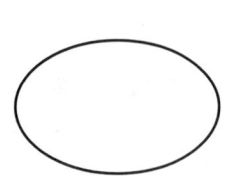 d.

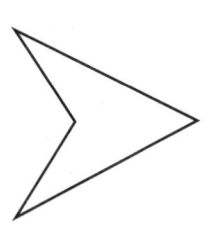

   _____ _____ _____ _____

2. A circle has an infinite number of lines of symmetry. Draw different lines of symmetry on these four circles.

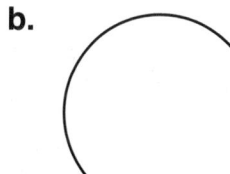

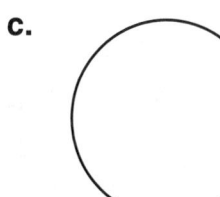

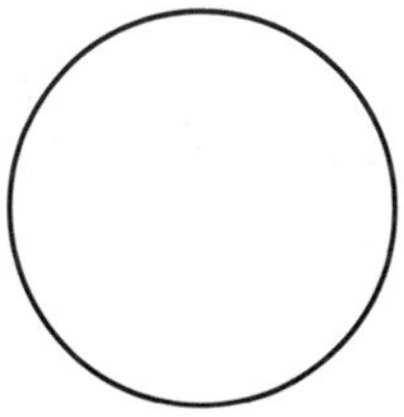

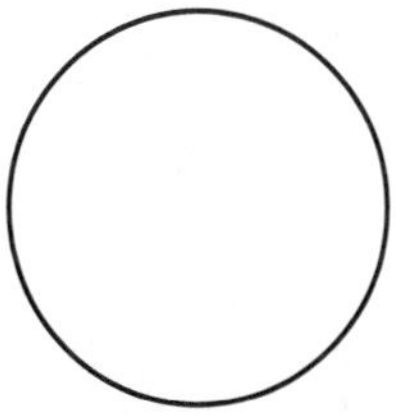

   a. 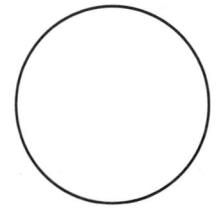 b. c. d.

   2 lines 6 lines 1 line 10 lines

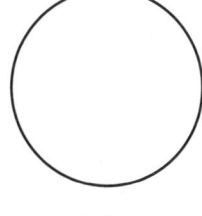

3. Color the pictures and shapes that are symmetrical.

   a. 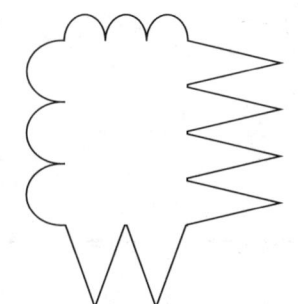 b. 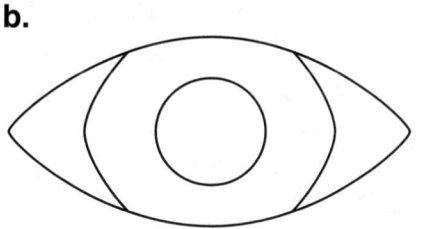 c.

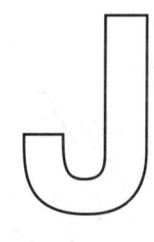

   d.

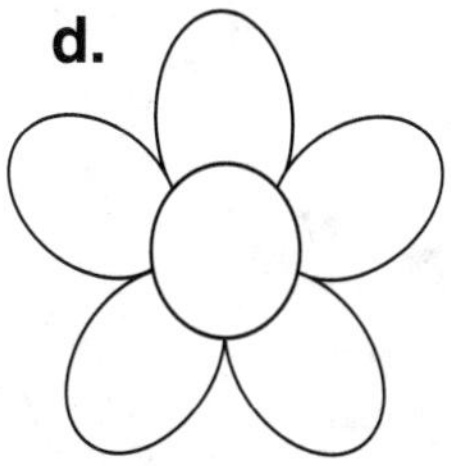

   e.

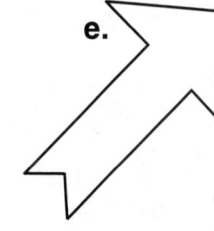

   f.

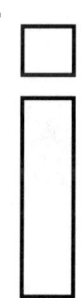

   g.  h.

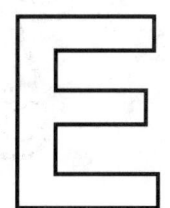

61

© Teacher Created Resources, Inc. #8995 Targeting Math: Geometry, Chance and Data

Transformation and Symmetry

More Lines of Symmetry

Name   **Date**

1. Draw a line of symmetry through each of these letters.

   a. B   b. D   c. T   d. i   e. C

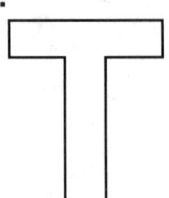

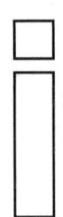

2. How many lines of symmetry do the shapes below have? Use a ruler to help you draw the line or lines on each shapes. Then write the number of lines you drew below the shapes.

   a.   b.   c.   d.

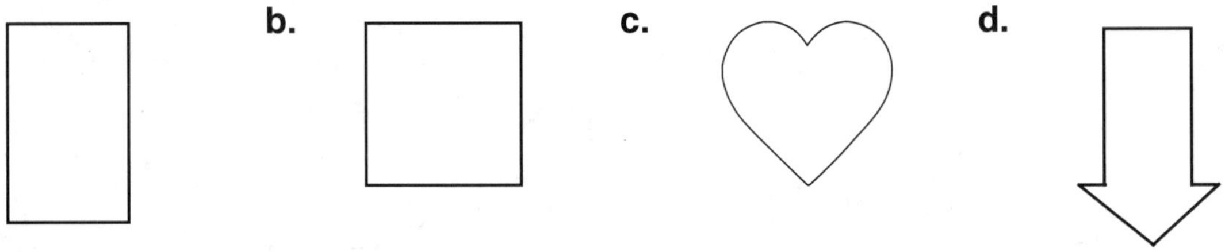

   e.   f.   g.   h.

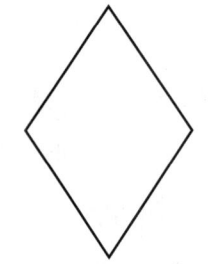

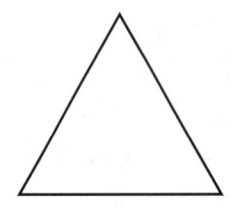

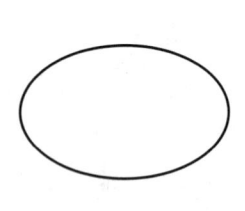

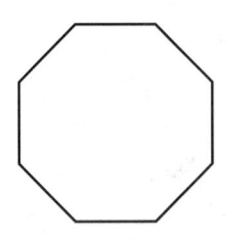

3. Draw the other half of each picture across the line of symmetry.

   a.   b.

#8995 Targeting Math: Geometry, Chance and Data   © Teacher Created Resources, Inc.

Transformation and Symmetry

Patterns

Name **Date**

1. Draw a shape. Create a pattern by sliding your shape. Then color your pattern.

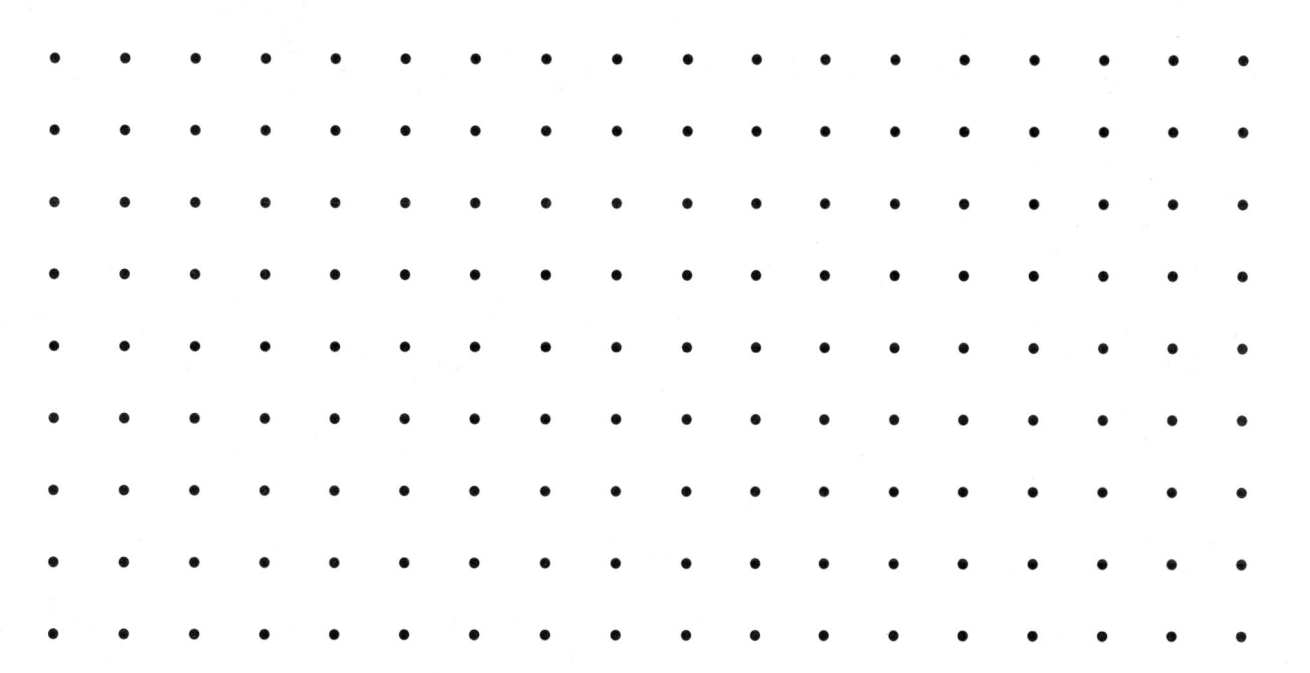

2. Draw a different shape. This time make a pattern by flipping your shape. Then color your pattern.

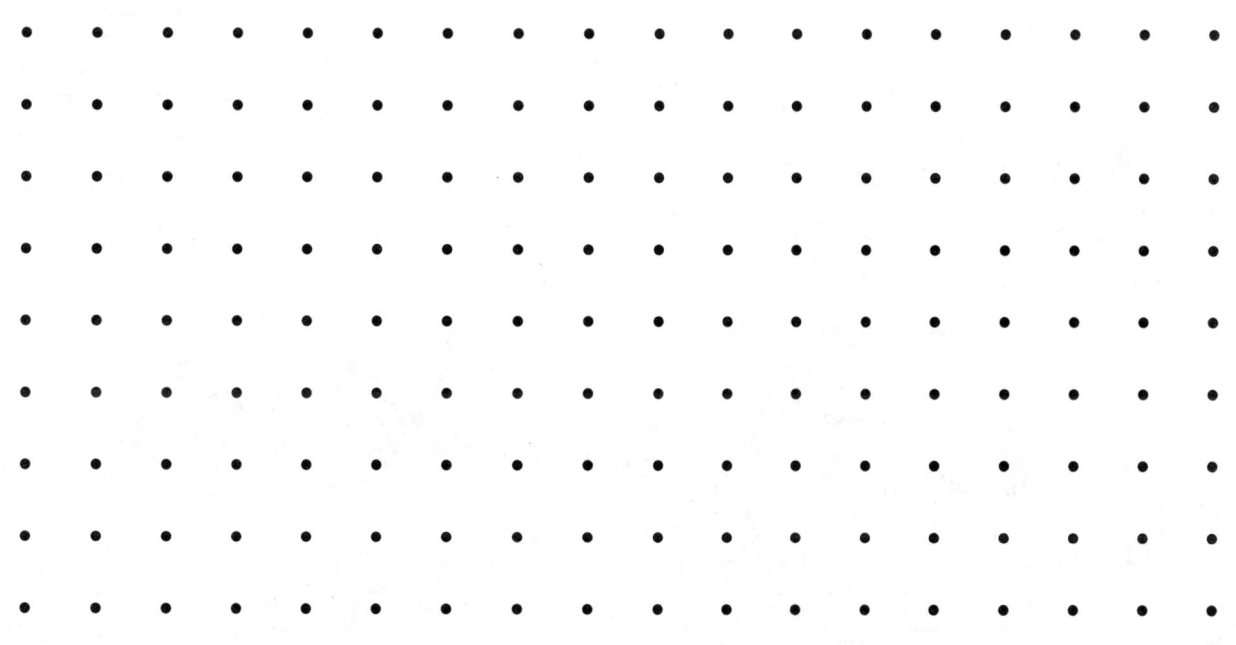

63

© Teacher Created Resources, Inc. #8995 Targeting Math: Geometry, Chance and Data

Transformation and Symmetry   Assessment

Name   **Date**

1. Complete the table.

Shape	Flip	Slide	Turn
a. 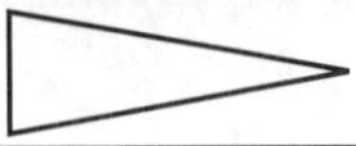			
b. 			
c. 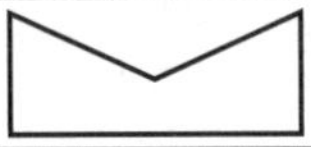			

2. Draw a line of symmetry through each shape.

   a.   b.   c.   d.

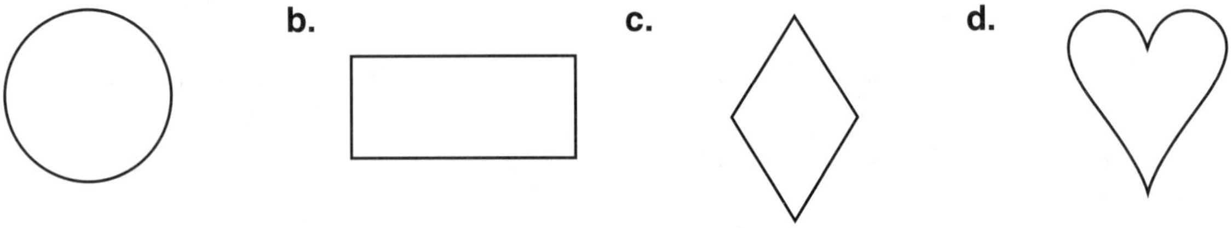

3. How many lines of symmetry do these shapes have? Draw them.

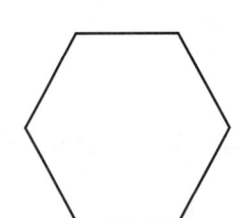

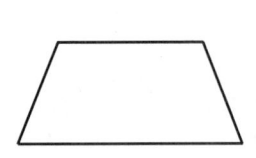

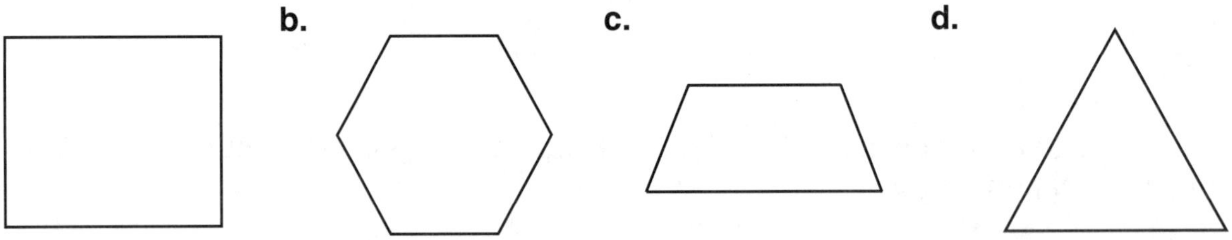

   a.   b.   c.   d.

   _____   _____   _____   _____

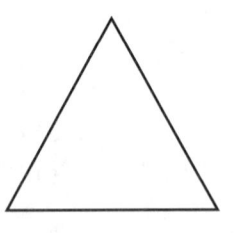

4. Complete the symmetrical drawings.

   a.   b.

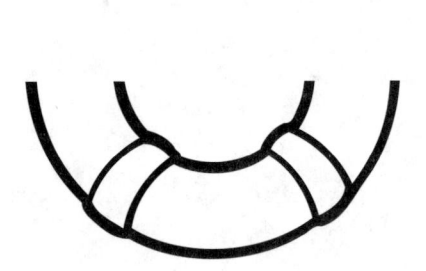

5. Continue this pattern.

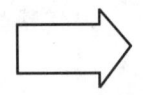

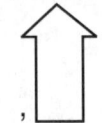

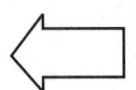

   ⇒ , ⇑ , ⇐ , _____ , _____ , _____ , _____

(64)

#8995 Targeting Math: Geometry, Chance and Data   © Teacher Created Resources, Inc.

Transformation and Symmetry

Name   **Date**

Activity Page

1. All the symbols below look strange! Work out the next symbol in each group.
   (Hint: turning the page might help.)

   a.

   b.

2. Trace over this pattern to make a cardboard tile. Complete the grid by turning and flipping the tile. Color your pattern and cut it out. Stick it on cardboard to make a greeting card.

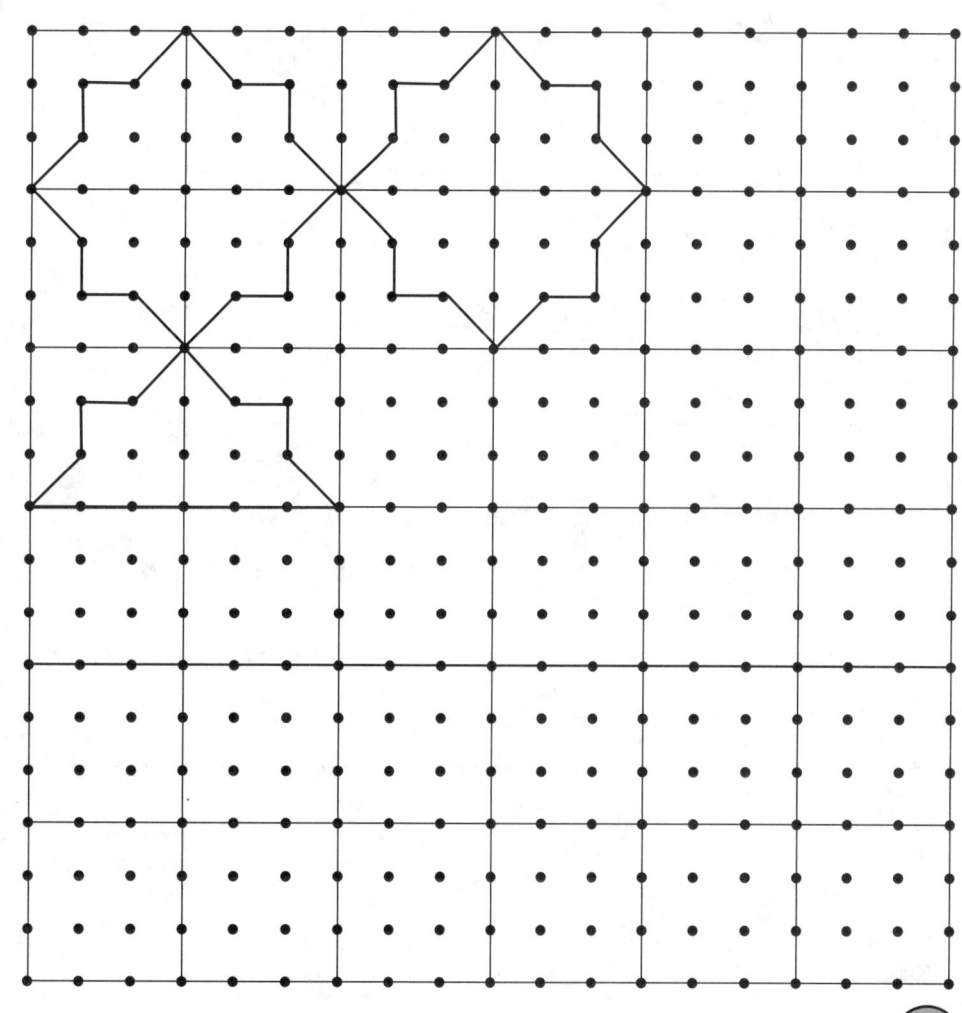

© Teacher Created Resources, Inc.   #8995 Targeting Math: Geometry, Chance and Data

Transformation and Symmetry

Name **Date**

Activity Page

Circle the one that is the exact opposite to the first one.

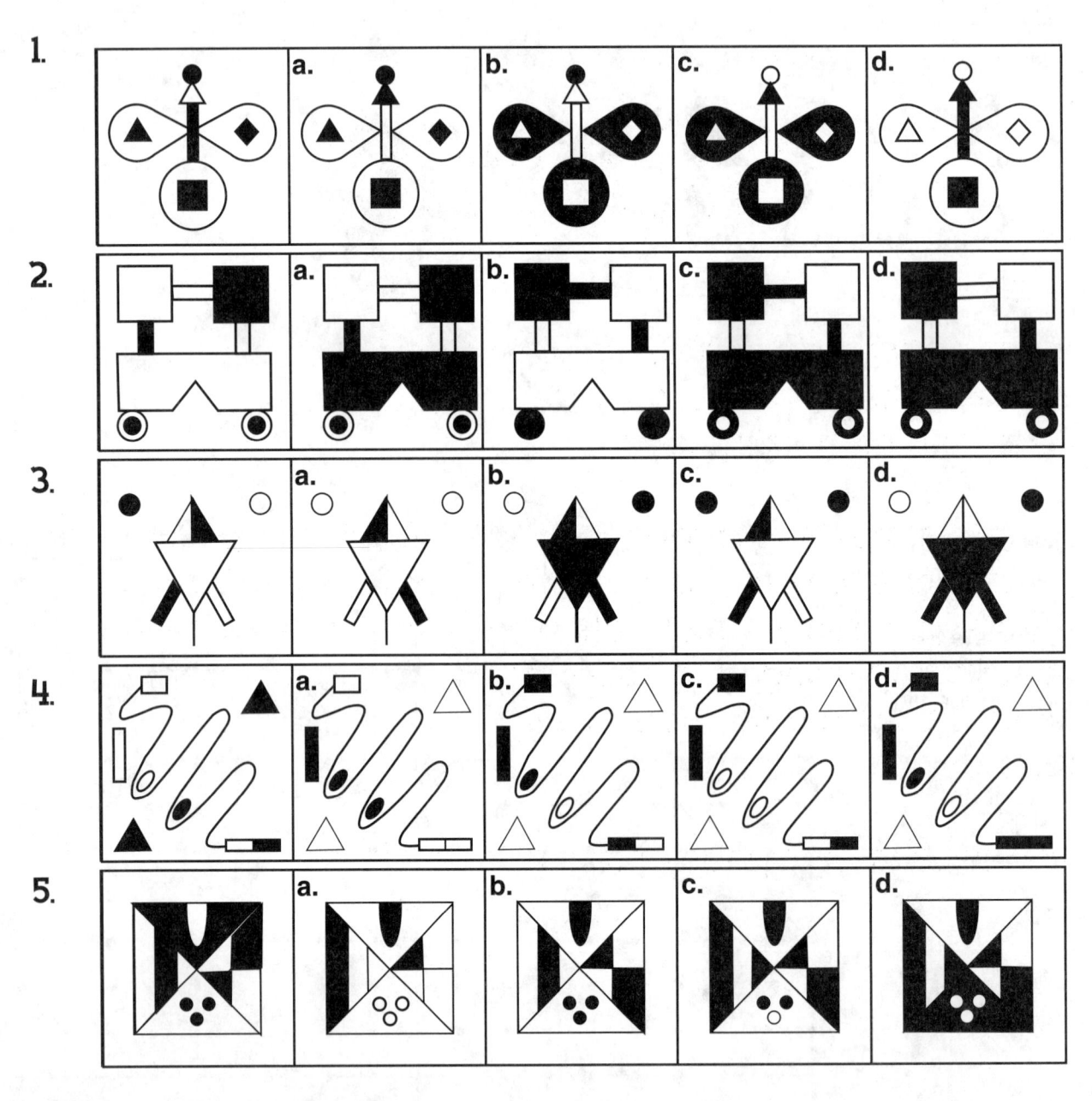

1.

2.

3.

4.

5.

Now draw one of your own.

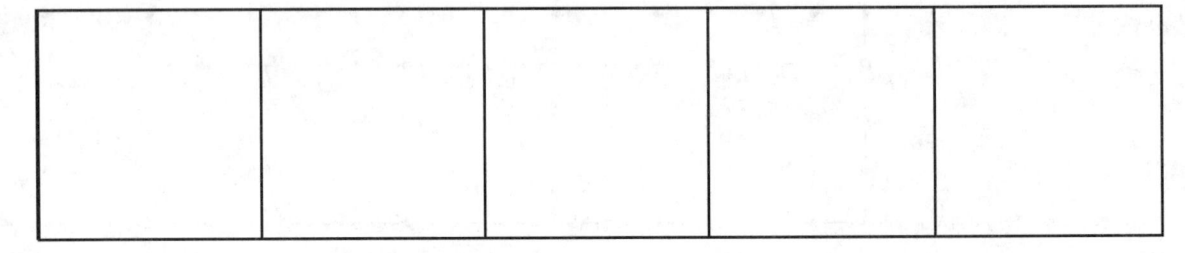

GRAPHS

In these two units, students practice skills in conducting surveys, recording, summarizing, representing collected data, and organizing data.

Students must interpret and locate information using picture, line, column, bar, and pie graphs. Tally marks are used to record information collected. Graphs are constructed using data collected by the students as well as using given data. The activity page uses graphs in a fun way.

Two assessment pages are included.

GRAPHS

Unit 1

Recording Information
Tally Marks
Picture Graph
Column Graph
Bar Graph
Problem Solving

Objectives
- display, read and interpret a variety of graphs
- gather, organize, display, and interpret data and present findings in a column graph or bar graph
- summarize data based on tallying or organized lists
- check whether answers to problems are correct and sensible

Language
tally, column, graph, bar, results, title, data, line, horizontal, vertical, survey, represent, picture, results

Materials/Resources
ruler, blank paper, colored pencils, dice, calculator

Contents of Student Pages
* materials needed for each reproducible student page

Page 70 Tally Marks
recording results using tally marks; graphing results
* colored pencils

Page 71 Picture Graphs
survey class; record results; construct a picture graph

Page 72 Column Graphs
record experiment results; draw a column graph
* calculator

Page 73 Problem Solvings
using horizontal and vertical column graphs
* calculator

Page 74 Line Graphs
reading a line graph; drawing a line graph; drawing a line graph from given information

Page 75 Bar Graphs
horizontal column graph; problem solving using a bar graph.

Page 76 Assessment
Page 77 Activity
two graphing activities

Remember

Before starting, ensure that each student:
- ❑ develops the habit of checking all work.
- ❑ is encouraged to use a ruler when constructing graphs.
- ❑ understands the difference between column graphs and bar graphs.

#8995 Targeting Math: Geometry, Chance and Data © Teacher Created Resources, Inc.

Additional Activities
- ❏ Have students conduct their own surveys and complete tables showing results.
- ❏ Collect graphs from magazines, etc. Display them in a class chart, on a poster, or in a class graph book.
- ❏ Have students draw their own graphs and write questions about them. They then swap with partners to answer one another's questions.

Answers

Page 70 Tally Marks
Check individual work.

Page 71 Picture Graph
Check individual work.

Page 72 Column Graph
Check individual work.

Page 73 Problem Solving
1. a. Sam
   b. Anne
   c. Amy and Lyn, Ben and Tim
   d. 14 lbs
   e. 61 lbs
   d. 733 lbs
2. Check individual work.

Page 74 Line Graphs
1. a. Stan
   b. Molly
   c. Charlie and Matthew
   d. 44 hours

Page 75 Bar Graphs
1. Check individual work.
2. a. grapes
   b. mangoes
   c. apples and oranges
   d. own answer

Page 76 Assessment
1. Check individual work.
2. a. Silver
   b. Black and Red
   c. 20
   d. 80

Page 77 Activity
1. b
2. a. Kevin
   b. cross out
   c. Jan
   d. 36
   e. cross out
   f. cross out
   g. cross out
   h. 2

Graphs   Tally Marks

Name   **Date**

1. Find out how many children are in each of your classmates' families. Complete the table below. Use tally marks to record the results of the survey.

Number of Children	Tally	Total
1		
2		
3		
4		
other		

2. Color one square to represent each family.

Number of Children   **Number of Families**

1
2
3
4
other

3. Draw a picture of your family.

Graphs

Picture Graph

Name   **Date**

1. Survey the class to find out the pets that each family owns. Tally and total the results. Then construct a picture graph below.

a.

Pets	Tally	Total
dogs		
cats		
birds		
fish		
mice		
others		

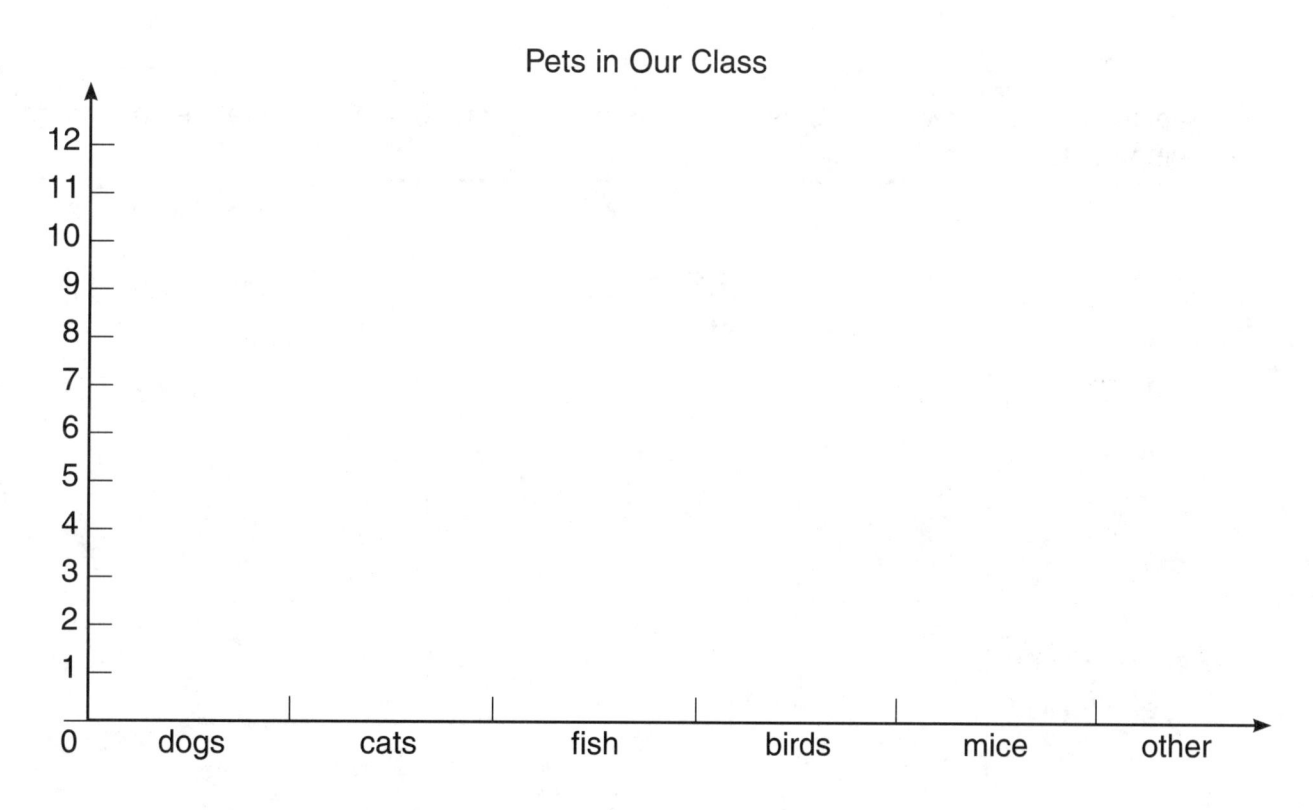

b.   Pets in Our Class

(Graph with y-axis labeled 0–12 and x-axis labels: dogs, cats, fish, birds, mice, other)

c. What was the most popular pet in the class? _____

d. What was the total number of pets? _____

e. Were there any unusual pets? If so, what were they? _____
_____

71

© Teacher Created Resources, Inc.   #8995 Targeting Math: Geometry, Chance and Data

Graphs   Column Graph

Name   **Date**

1. Work with a partner.
   a. Flip a coin 30 times. Color a square to record each result.

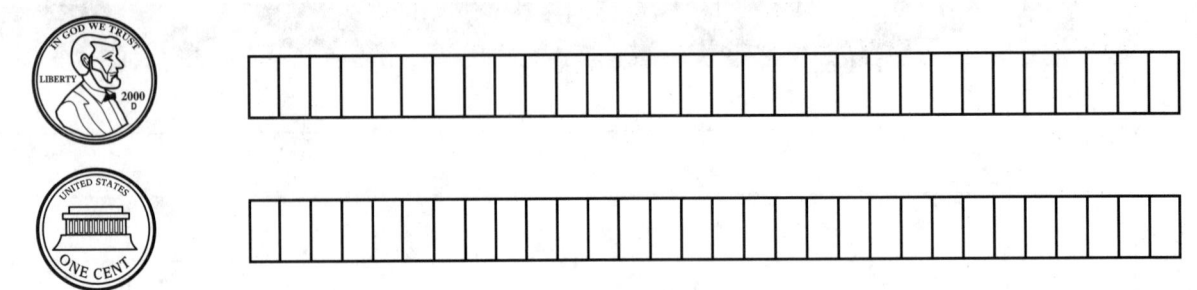

   b. Which occurred most often? _____

   c. Did every group have the same result? _____

2. Teachers were surveyed and asked about their favorite fruit. Complete the column graph using these results.

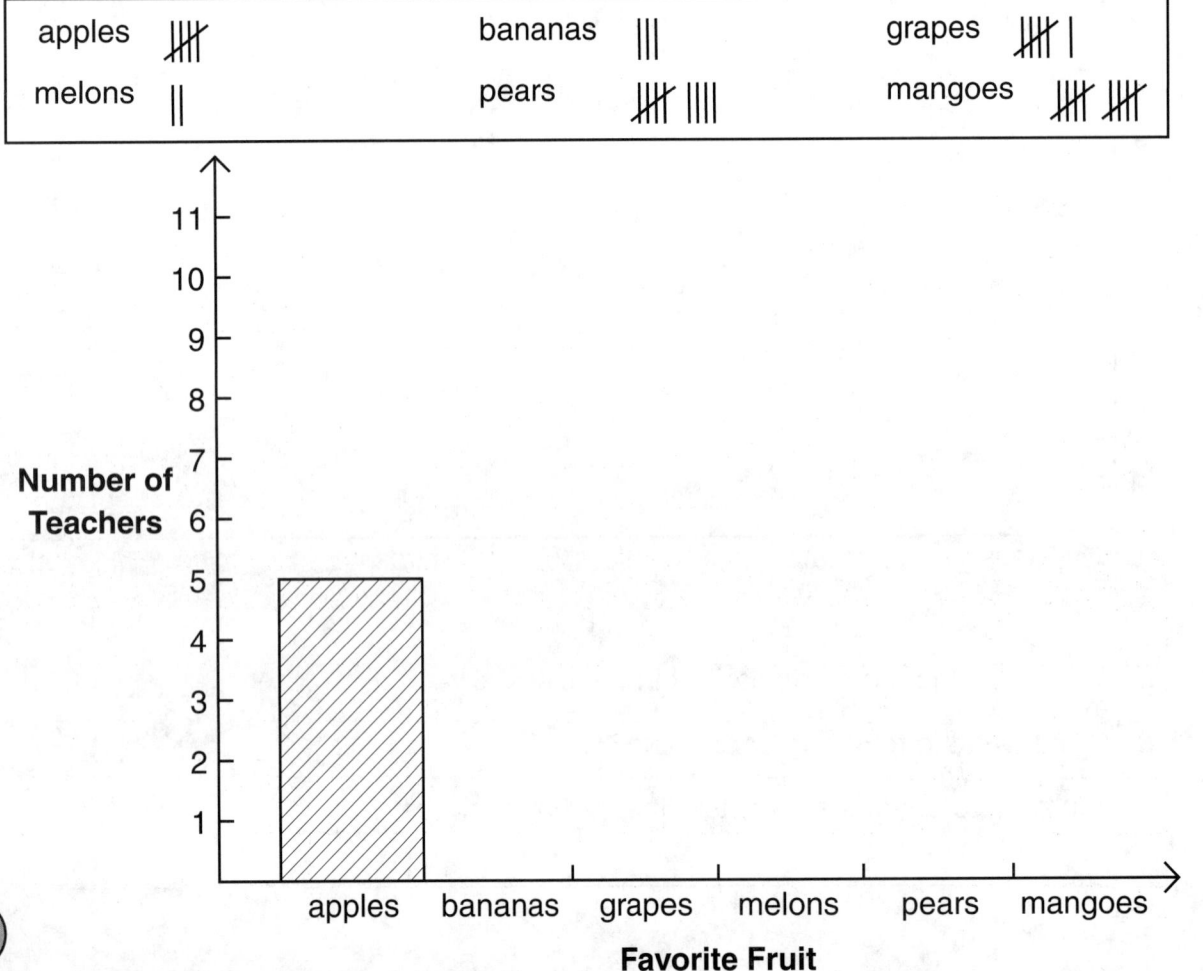

   | apples | |||| | bananas | ||| | grapes | |||| | |
   | melons | || | pears | |||| |||| | mangoes | |||| |||| |

   Number of Teachers

   Favorite Fruit

#8995 Targeting Math: Geometry, Chance and Data   © Teacher Created Resources, Inc.

Graphs   Problem Solving

Name   **Date**

1. This graph shows the weights of 11 fourth-grade students. Look at the data and answer the questions.

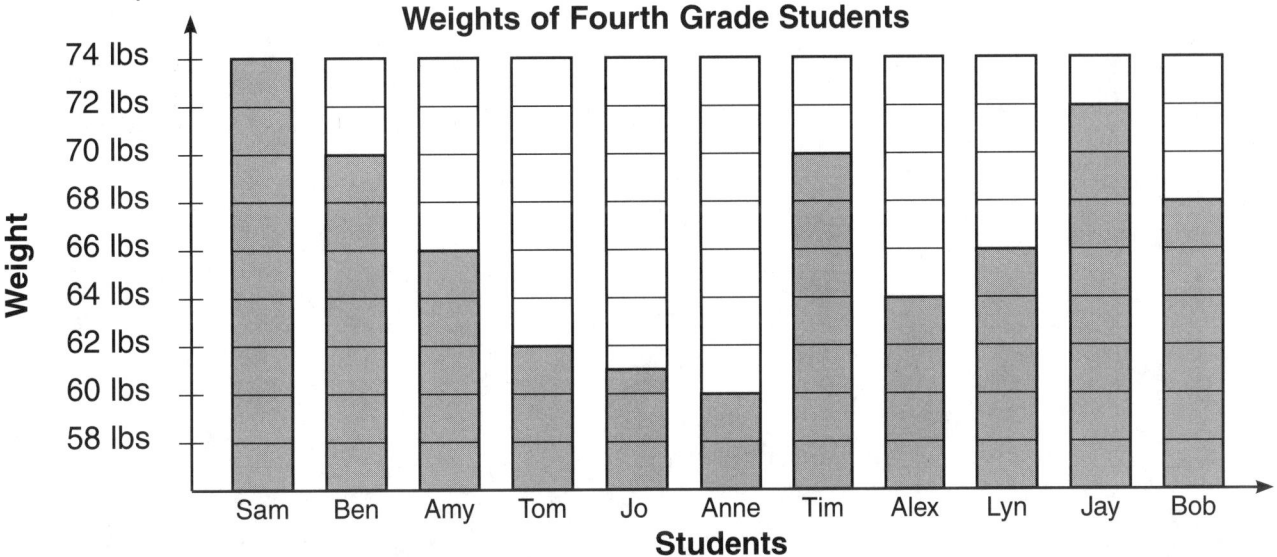

   Weights of Fourth Grade Students

   Weight (y-axis): 58 lbs to 74 lbs
   Students (x-axis): Sam, Ben, Amy, Tom, Jo, Anne, Tim, Alex, Lyn, Jay, Bob

   a. Who was the heaviest in the class? _____
   b. Who was the lightest in the class? _____
   c. Which children weighed the same amount? _____
   d. What was the difference between the lightest and heaviest child? _____
   e. How much did Jo weigh? _____
   f. Use a calculator and find the total weight of the eleven children. _____

2. This graph shows how many books each child read during the term. Look at the graph and complete the data in tally form.

   Key ▨ = 2 books

   Sarah
   Jake
   Mary
   Steve
   David

Name	Tally	Total

Graphs   Line Graph

Name   **Date**

1. The line graph below shows how many hours of television a group of children watch. Use the information to answer the questions.

Watching Television

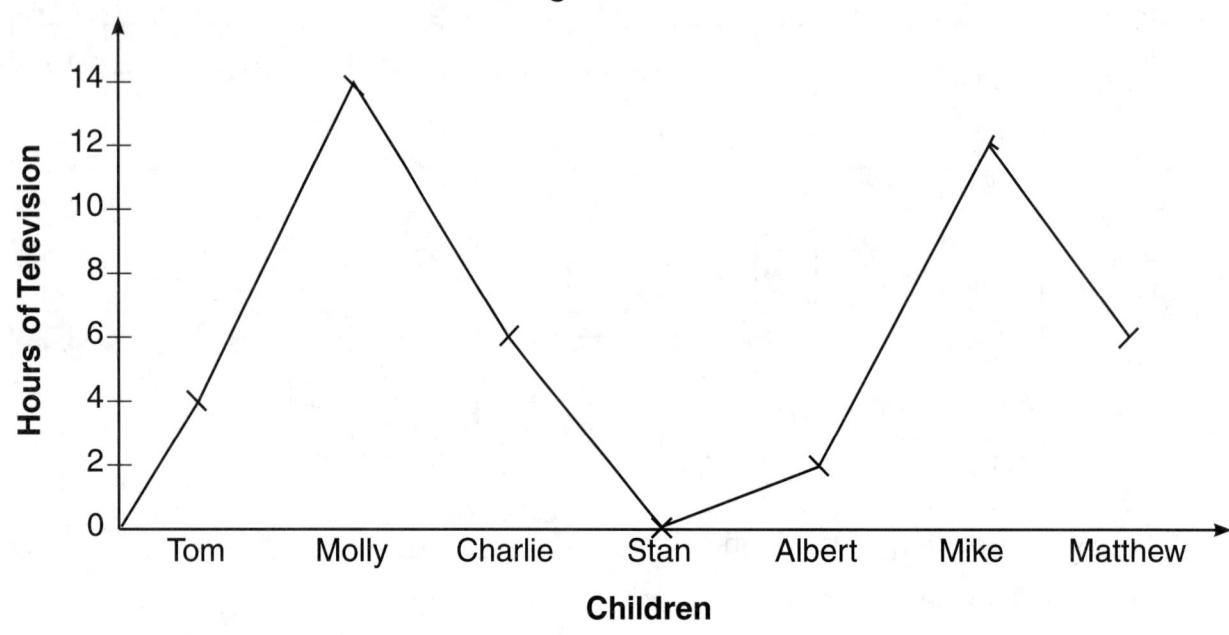

Hours of Television (y-axis: 0, 2, 4, 6, 8, 10, 12, 14)

Tom 4, Molly 14, Charlie 6, Stan 0, Albert 2, Mike 12, Matthew 6

Children

   a. Who doesn't watch any television? _____

   b. Who watches the most television in the group? _____

   c. Who watches the same amount of television? _____

   d. What was the total amount of hours watched? _____

2. Use the information below to draw a line graph. Remember the labels!
   In the class spelling test, these were the results: **Tim 16, Sally, 18, Casey 11, Fiona 13, Sasha 11, Toby 14, Daniel 15, Todd 12.**

Graphs   *Bar Graph*

Name   **Date**

1. Robert had a car washing business. Complete the column graph for him, based on the data he collected during a one week period.

Days of the Week	Tally of Cars Washed	Total
Monday	||||	
Tuesday	|||| |	
Wednesday	|||| |||	
Thursday	|||| ||||	
Friday	||	
Saturday	|||| |||| ||||	
Sunday	|||| |||| |||| ||||	

Key ▨ = 1

2. Answer the questions below. The information below shows how much fruit was sold in a day at the school snack bar.

[bar: apples | mangoes | bananas | grapes | oranges]

    a. What was the most popular fruit sold? _____

    b. What was the least popular fruit sold? _____

    c. Which fruits had the same popularity? _____

    d. Which fruit would you have bought? _____

© Teacher Created Resources, Inc.   #8995 Targeting Math: Geometry, Chance and Data

Graphs   Assessment

Name   **Date**

1. Look at the information below. Draw horizontal and vertical graphs to represent the data. Children were surveyed about their favorite sports.

Sports	Tally	Total
Football	||||		
Soccer	|||| |||	
Tennis	|||	
Swimming	||	
Basketball	|||| ||||		
Running	||||		

a.

football
soccer
tennis
swimming
basketball
running

b.

football   soccer   tennis   swimming   basketball   running

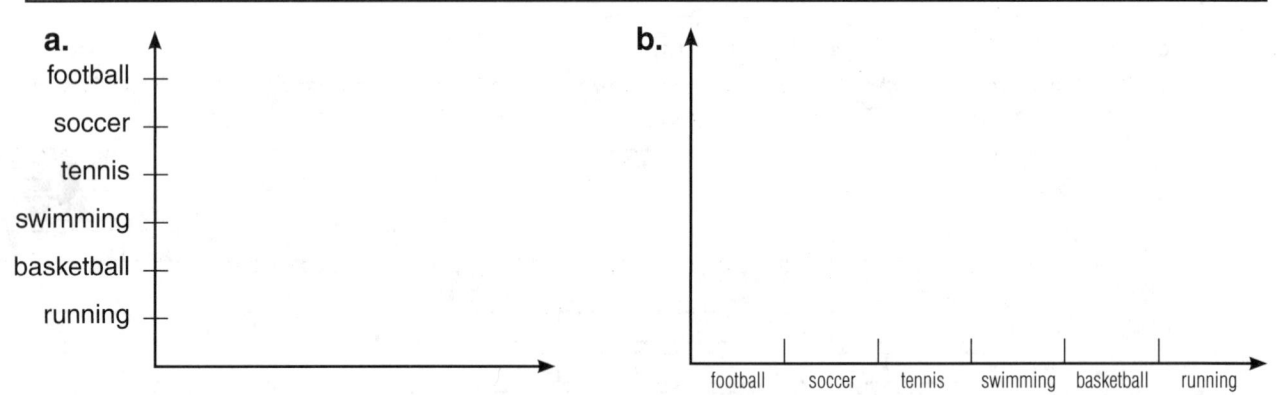

2. A group of children were surveyed about their favorite colors of cars. Study the graph and answer the questions.

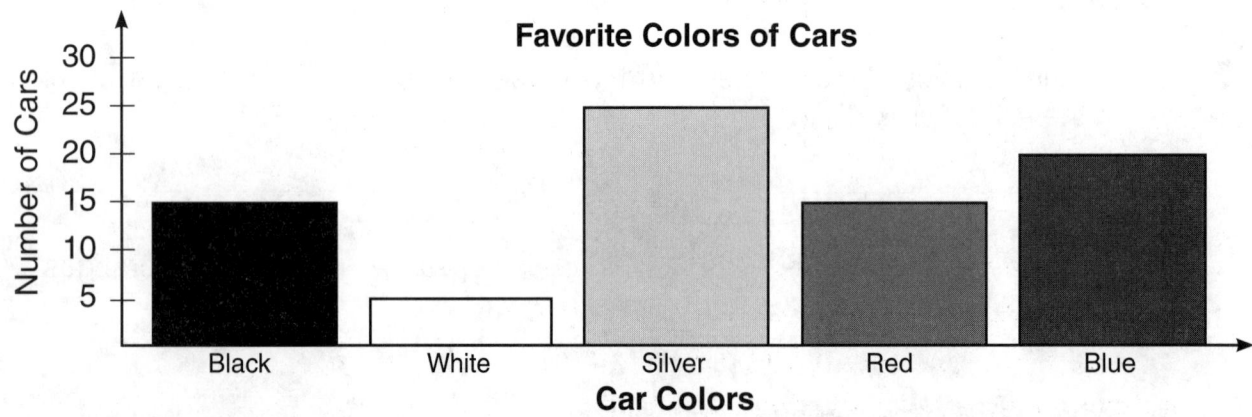

Favorite Colors of Cars

Number of Cars: 30, 25, 20, 15, 10, 5

Black — 15
White — 5
Silver — 25
Red — 15
Blue — 20

Car Colors

a. What was the most popular car? _____
b. Which cars had the same amount of popularity? _____
c. How many children voted for Blue? _____
d. How many children were surveyed? _____

Graphs   Activity Page

Name   **Date**

Graphs

1. Only one of these graphs is correct. Circle the one which shows the following information: Spoks have 20 teeth, Goks have 10 teeth, Toks have 30 teeth.

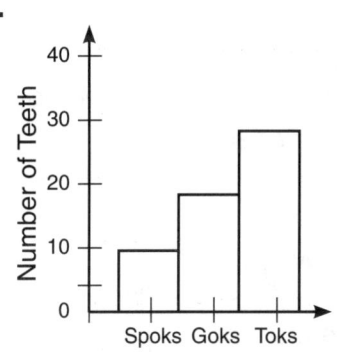

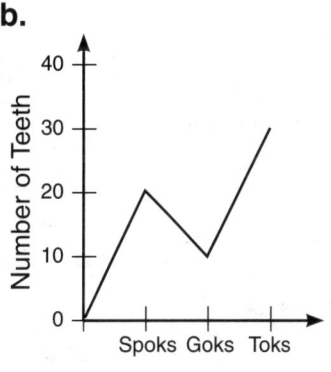

   a. [bar graph: Spoks ~10, Goks ~18, Toks ~28; y-axis Number of Teeth 0–40]

   b. [line graph: Spoks ~20, Goks ~10, Toks ~30; y-axis Number of Teeth 0–40]

   c. Number of Teeth
      | Goks | Toks | Spoks |

2. You can't tell everything from a graph. Answer all the questions you can. Draw a line through any question you cannot answer from the graph.

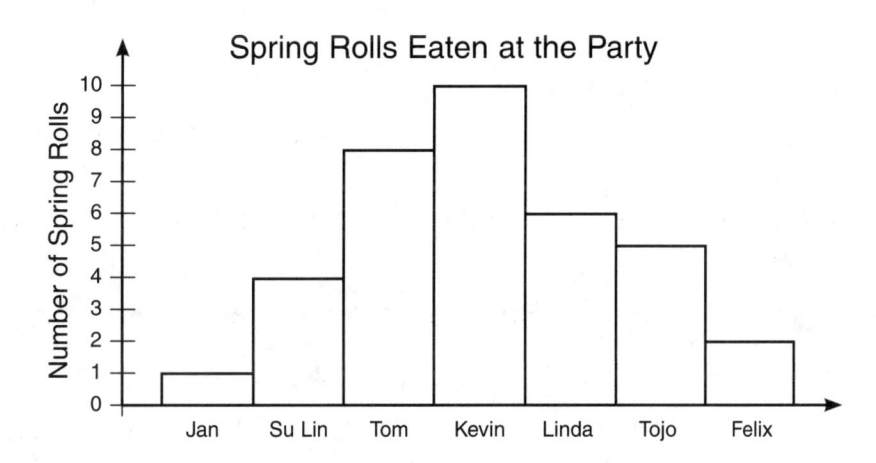

   Spring Rolls Eaten at the Party

   [bar graph, Number of Spring Rolls 0–10: Jan 1, Su Lin 4, Tom 8, Kevin 10, Linda 6, Tojo 5, Felix 2]

   a. Who ate the most spring rolls? _____
   b. How many people were at the party? _____
   c. Which girl ate the least number of spring rolls? _____
   d. How many were eaten altogether? _____
   e. Were they vegetarian spring rolls? _____
   f. Do you think Kevin liked spring rolls? _____
   g. How long did it take Jan to eat her spring roll? _____
   h. How many more did Linda eat than Su Lin? _____

   © Teacher Created Resources, Inc.   #8995 Targeting Math: Geometry, Chance and Data

GRAPHS

Unit 2

Surveys
Tally
Picture Graphs
Column Graphs
Bar Graphs
Line Graphs
Pie Graphs

Objectives
- display, read, and interpret a variety of graphs
- gather, organize, display and interpret data and present findings in a column graph or bar graph
- summarize data based on tallying or organized lists
- check whether answers to problems are correct and sensible

Language
tally, column, graph, bar, results, title, data, line, column, horizontal, vertical, survey, pie, represent, picture, results

Materials/Resources
ruler, blank paper, colored pencils, dice, calculator

Contents of Student Pages
* materials needed for each reproducible student page

Page 80 Traffic Survey
horizontal column graph, vertical column graph

Page 81 Picture Graph
experiment with dice, draw a column graph, interpret a picture graph
* dice

Page 82 Bar Graphs
interpreting a bar graph; gathering information; constructing a bar graph

Page 83 More Graphs
reading and interpreting, constructing graphs

Page 84 Pie Graphs
interpreting information
* colored pencils

Page 85 Line Graphs
answering questions on information shown

Page 86 Assessment
* colored pencils

Remember

Before starting, ensure that each student:
- ❑ understands the importance of neatly showing all work.
- ❑ develops the habit of checking.
- ❑ is encouraged to use a ruler when constructing graphs.

Additional Activities

❑ Have students who need extension activities start drawing pie graphs using protractors.

❑ Collect many examples of different types of graphs. Have each student present one graph to the class. He or she can then tell the other students about it and answer their questions.

❑ Make display charts of different types of graphs. The graphs from the previous activity can be used.

❑ Working in small groups, students can design and carry out their own surveys. The results can be graphed in three different ways. These graphs can then be explained to the class.

Answers

Page 80 Traffic Survey
1. Check individual work.
2. a. Friday
   b. Wednesday
   c. 14 children
   d. 6

Page 81 Picture Graphs
1. Check individual work.
2. a. star ☆
   b. rectangle ☐
   c. 15
   d. 20
   e. own choice

Page 82 Bar Graphs
1. a. Native Countries of School Children
   b. Australia
   c. Britain
   d. 150
   e. 6
   f. Check individual work.
2. Check individual work.

Page 83 More Graphs
1. a. 50
   b. Orchids
   c. 210
   d. 60
   e. Check individual work.
2. Check individual work.

Page 84 Pie Graphs
1. a. blue
   b. gold
   c. red and yellow
   d. purple
   e. Check individual work.
   f. red, purple, green or yellow, blue, gold
2. a. classical and jazz
   b. heavy metal
   c. $\frac{1}{4}$
   d. classical and jazz
   e. own choice

Page 85 Line Graphs
1. a. $2
   b. $6
   c. $3\frac{1}{2}$ lbs
   d. $\frac{1}{2}$ lb
   e. $2\frac{1}{2}$ lbs
   f. $7.00
2. a. Saturday, Sunday
   b. Monday
   c. Sunday
   d. 460 videos

Page 86 Assessment
1. a. milk
   b. 10 children
   c. 10
   d. Check individual work.
2. Check individual work.

Graphs   Traffic Survey

Name	Date

1. Survey the traffic that passes your school for 20 minutes. Tally the results and graph them on a horizontal column graph.

Vehicles	Tally	Total
car		
truck		
bicycle		
bus		
walk		
other		

- car
- truck
- bicycle
- bus
- walkers
- other

2. This vertical column graph is a survey of children who were away from River Road Public School during one week. Answer the questions.

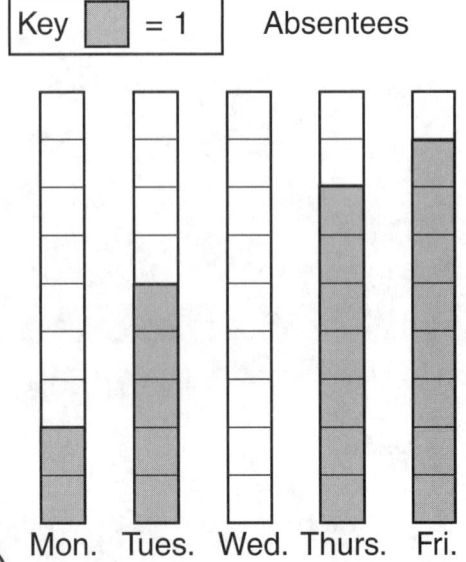

Key ▢ = 1   Absentees

Mon. Tues. Wed. Thurs. Fri.

a. On which day had the highest number of absentees? _____

b. On which day did everyone come to school? _____

c. How many children were away on Monday, Tuesday and Thursday? _____

d. What was the difference between the number of absentees on Friday and Monday? _____

#8995 Targeting Math: Geometry, Chance and Data   © Teacher Created Resources, Inc.

Graphs   Picture Graphs

Name　　　　　　　　　　　　　　　　　**Date**

1. Throw a die 30 times. Tally the results and then graph them on the vertical column graph.

Dice	Tally	Total
⚀		
⚁		
⚂		
⚃		
⚄		
⚅		

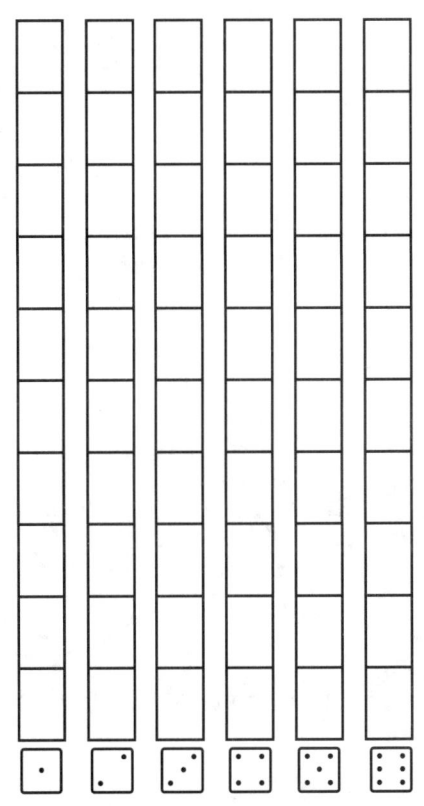

2. Children were asked about their favorite shapes. The picture graph below shows what their responses were. Use the picture graph to answer the questions.

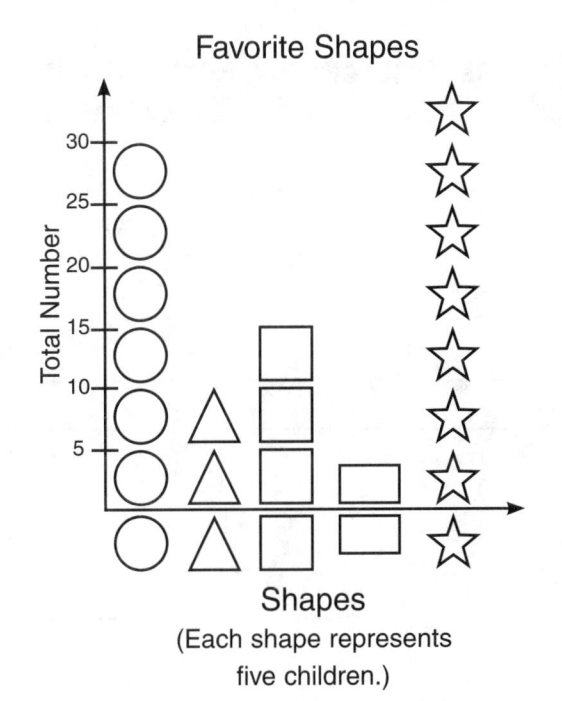

Favorite Shapes

(Each shape represents five children.)

a. What was the most popular shape?
_____

b. What was the least popular shape?
_____

c. How many children chose the square?
_____

d. What was the difference between the number of people who chose the stars and the squares? _____

e. What is your favorite shape?
_____

© Teacher Created Resources, Inc.   #8995 Targeting Math: Geometry, Chance and Data

Graphs

Bar Graphs

Name   **Date**

1. The information shows the nationalities of children who attend a local school in Australia. Look at the graph and answer the following questions.

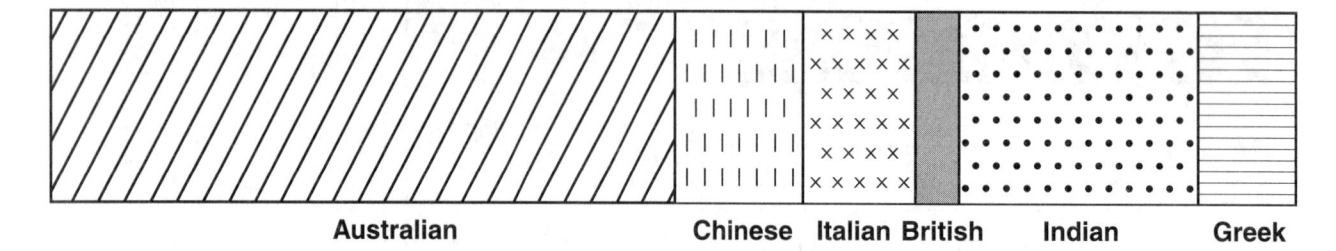

| Australian | Chinese | Italian | British | Indian | Greek |

a. Label the graph. _____

b. Where were most of the children born? _____

c. Where were the least number of children born? _____

d. If there were 300 children at the school, about how many were Australian? _____

e. How many countries are represented? _____

f. List the different countries represented in your class.

_____

2. Survey children in your class about the color of their hair. Tally the results. Draw a graph like the one above to show the results. Remember the labels!

Hair Color	Tally	Total
blonde		
brown		
red		
black		

#8995 Targeting Math: Geometry, Chance and Data   © Teacher Created Resources, Inc.

Graphs   *More Graphs*

Name   **Date**

1. Some local gardeners were asked about their favorite flowering plants. This graph was drawn. Answer the questions below.

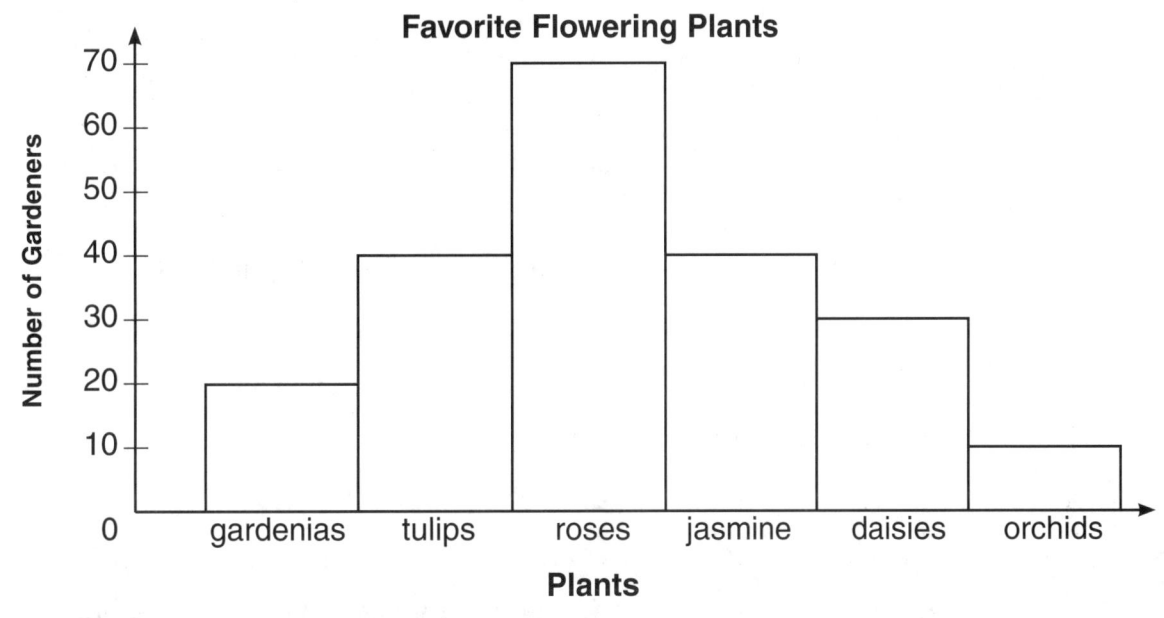

Favorite Flowering Plants

(Bar graph: gardenias 20, tulips 40, roses 70, jasmine 40, daisies 30, orchids 10)

Y-axis: Number of Gardeners
X-axis: Plants

a. How many gardeners chose daisies and gardenias? _____
b. Which was the least popular flowering plant? _____
c. How many gardeners were surveyed altogether? _____
d. What was the difference between the most and least popular plants?
_____

e. Why do you think roses were the most popular plant?
_____

2. A number of families were asked about their favorite cereals. On the back of this sheet draw a graph to show the results. Include all the labels.

Cereal	Tally	Total
Cornflakes™	|||| |||| ||||	
Nutrigrain™	|||| |||| ||	
Mueslix™	|||	
Fruit Loops™	|||| |||	
Rice Krispies™	||||	

Graphs

Pie Graphs

Name _____ **Date** _____

1. Children were asked what their favorite color was. Look at the pie graph for the results and answer the questions.

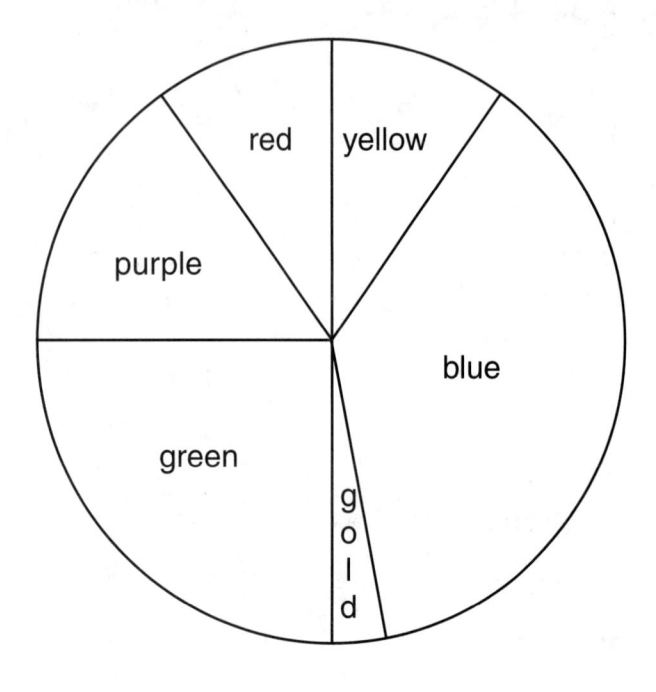

   a. What was the most popular color?
   _____

   b. What was the least popular color?
   _____

   c. Which two colors had the same popularity?
   _____

   d. Which color had twice the popularity of red?
   _____

   e. Color the pie graph to make the results clearer.

   f. Name three colors which make up half the numbers. _____
   _____

2. A group of adults was asked about their favorite music. Look at the pie graph for the results and answer the questions.

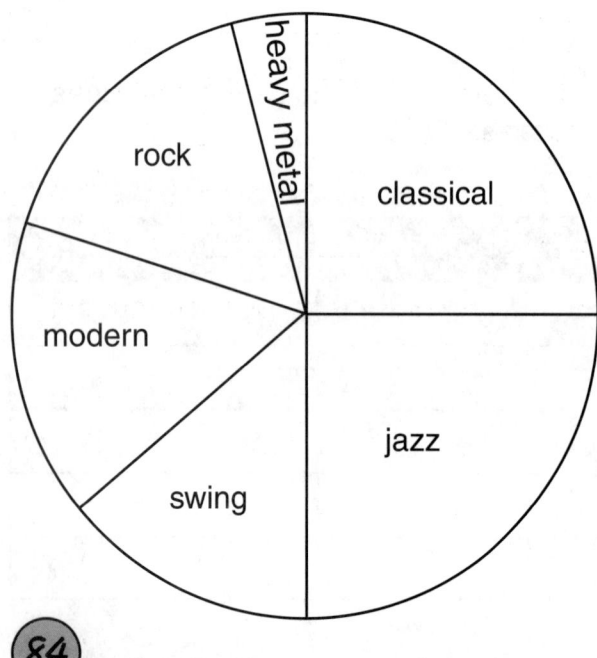

   a. Which were the two most popular types of music? _____

   b. Which was the least popular type of music?
   _____

   c. What fraction of the total music selection was jazz? _____

   d. Which two types of music make up half the total? _____

   e. What is your favorite type of music?
   _____

84

#8995 Targeting Math: Geometry, Chance and Data © Teacher Created Resources, Inc.

Graphs   Line Graphs

Name   **Date**

1. This line graph shows the cost of grapes. Look at it and answer the questions.

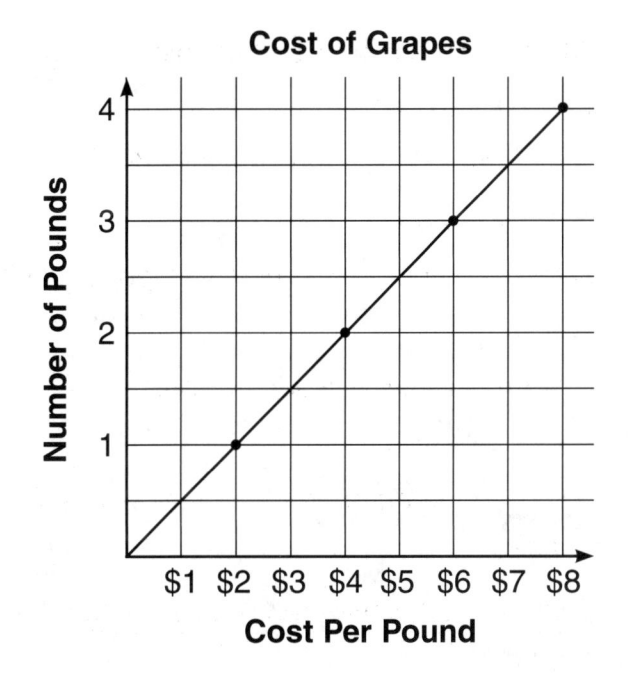

Cost of Grapes

(graph: Number of Pounds vs Cost Per Pound, line passing through ($1,1), ($2,1), ($4,2), ($6,3), ($8,4))

a. How much will 1 pound of grapes cost? _____

b. How much will 3 pounds of grapes cost? _____

c. Who many pounds of grapes could I buy for $7? _____

d. How many pounds of grapes could I buy for $1? _____

e. If I spent $5, what would my grapes weigh? _____

f. How much will it cost to buy 3 ½ pounds of grapes? _____

2. This line graph shows the number of videos borrowed over one week.

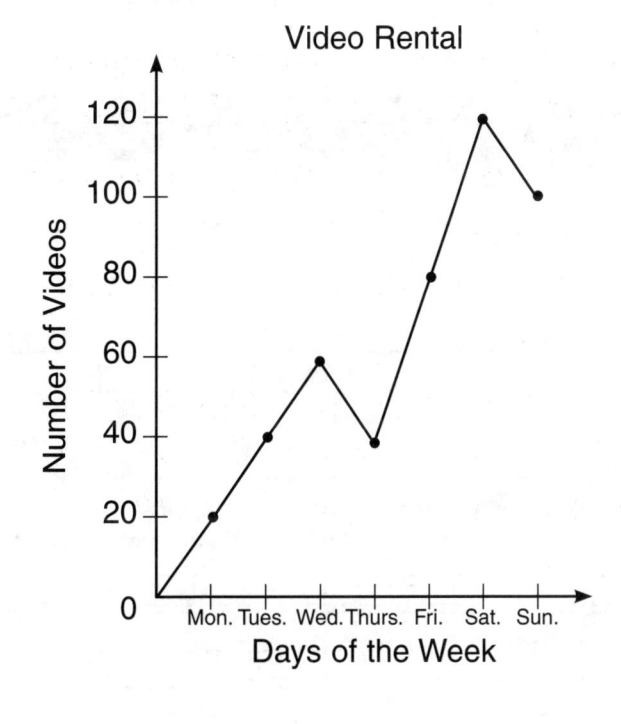

Video Rental

(graph: Number of Videos vs Days of the Week — Mon 20, Tues 40, Wed 60, Thurs 40, Fri 80, Sat 120, Sun 100)

a. What are the two busiest days at the video shop? _____

b. On which night was the least number of videos rented? _____

c. What day did the video shop rent out 100 videos? _____

d. How many videos did the shop rent out altogether? _____

© Teacher Created Resources, Inc.   #8995 Targeting Math: Geometry, Chance and Data

Graphs   Assessment

Name	Date

1. Forty children were surveyed about their favorite drinks. Look at the pie graph for the results and answer the questions.

   Favorite Drinks

   (pie graph with sections: water, cola, lemonade, milk, orange juice)

   a. Which was the most popular drink?
   _____

   b. How many children chose orange juice?
   _____

   c. What was the difference between the number of children who chose milk and those who chose orange juice? _____

   d. Make a bar graph from the information. Color the different sections to make the results clear.

2. Mr. Smith's class was asked what color their eyes are. Transfer the results from the data chart to the horizontal graph. Fill in the total column and then make a horizontal column graph to show the information. Give the graph a title.

Eye Color	Tally	Total
brown	IIII	
blue	H̶H̶ I	
green	H̶H̶ III	
hazel	II	
other	I	

brown
blue
green
hazel
other

#8995 Targeting Math: Geometry, Chance and Data   © Teacher Created Resources, Inc.

CHANCE AND DATA

The concept of an event being possible, impossible, or unlikely is explored in the units on Chance and Data.

Students must decide on possible paths, whether something is true or false, and chances of an event occurring. They practice recording different outcomes and listing possible outcomes. They carry out experiments and predict results.

Two assessment pages and a game of chance have been included.

© Teacher Created Resources, Inc. #8995 Targeting Math: Geometry, Chance and Data

CHANCE AND DATA

Unit 1

Chance
Probability
Certainty
Possible, Impossible
Likely, Unlikely
Combinations

Objectives

- record and identify all possible outcomes arising from simple chance experiments
- analyze situations and explain which events are possible, impossible, or certain to occur
- order easily understood events from least likely to most likely
- order easily understood events from least likely to most likely and justify choice
- compare own methods of solutions to problems with those of others
- explore different possibilities in familiar situations as an informal introduction to probability concepts
- make simple predictive statements about everyday events using the appropriate language of chance
- predict and validate the outcomes of simple probability experiments

Language

selection, choice, data, certain, certainty, possible, impossible, likely, unlikely, event, equal, chance

Materials/Resources

colored pencils, coins

Contents of Student Pages

* Materials needed for each reproducible student page

Page 90 Possibility
using the language certain, impossible, possible, likely, and unlikely; ordering events

Page 91 Possible Paths
showing different paths that can be followed
* colored pencils

Page 92 True or False
using true, false, or undecided to validate statements; making predictions

Page 93 Being Certain
recording outcomes by using pictures
* colored pencils

Page 94 Chances
using chance; working out odds
* coins, colored pencils

Page 95 Choices! Choices!
listing combinations and matching number sentences

Page 96 Assessment
Page 97 Activity
a game in which the winner is the first person through a maze

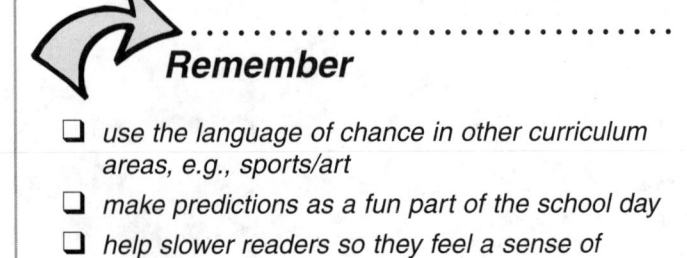

Remember

- use the language of chance in other curriculum areas, e.g., sports/art
- make predictions as a fun part of the school day
- help slower readers so they feel a sense of satisfaction in math
- explain the meaning of "event"

#8995 Targeting Math: Geometry, Chance and Data

© Teacher Created Resources, Inc.

Additional Activities

- ❏ Hold class discussions on gambling and odds in relation to chance.
- ❏ Have students research the largest lottery wins and write some problem-solving algorithms based on this information.
- ❏ Discuss the chances of winning a lottery. Have students collect lottery results from newspapers.
- ❏ Make a class book of sensible predictions. Review it regularly and check off those events that have occurred.
- ❏ Hold a class/grade raffle. Determine each entrant's chance of winning. Display this information before the raffle is drawn. Give students the opportunity to make their own predictions as to who they think will win and why.

Answers

Page 90 Possibility
1. a. possible
   b. possible
   c. possible
   d. certain
   e. impossible
   f. possible
   g. possible
   h. impossible
   i. certain
   j. certain
2. 4, 1, 3, 2
3. a. unlikely
   b. unlikely
   c. likely
   d. unlikely
   e. unlikely
   f. likely

Page 91 Possible Paths
Check individual work.

Page 92 True or False
1. a. unsure
   b. unsure
   c. false
   d. false
   e. false
   f. true
   g. true
   h. unsure
   i. false
   j. unsure
   k. unsure
   l. false
2. Check individual work.

Page 93 Being Certain
Check individual work.

Page 94 Chances
1. a. 1 chance out of 9
   b. 1 chance out of 8
   c. 14
   d. Check individual work.
   e. easier
   f. 12
2. Check individual work.

Page 95 Choices! Choices!
1. a. ham and lettuce
   b. ham and tomato
   c. ham and cheese
   d. cheese and tomato
   e. cheese and lettuce
   f. tomato and lettuce
2. Check individual work.
3. a. 2 x 2 x 3 = 12
   b. 2 x 3 x 4 = 24

Page 96 Assessment
1. Check individual work.
2. Check individual work.
3. a. 3 chances in 14
   b. 2 chances in 14
   c. 8 chances in 14
   d. 10 chances in 14
4. a. 4 x 2 = 8
   b. 2 x 3 = 6
   c. 2 x 3 x 2 = 12
5. Check individual work.

Chance and Data								Possibility

Name								**Date**

1. Read each of the events below. Decide whether they are **certain**, **possible**, or **impossible**.

    a. Tomorrow I will wear a hat. _____

    b. It rained today so yesterday was wet, too. _____

    c. My sister has a brother. _____

    d. My mother is older than I am. _____

    e. The last month of next year is April. _____

    f. Humans will walk on Mars. _____

    g. Cars will no longer run on gasoline. _____

    h. David's grandfather is younger than David. _____

    i. The hour after 11 o'clock A.M. is 12 o'clock P.M. _____

    j. Dairy cows give milk. _____

2. Order these events from **least likely** to **most likely**. Use numbers 1–4.

    a. Some adults use computers every day. _____

    b. No one will eat tomorrow. _____

    c. An artist will paint a picture of a boat. _____

    d. An earthquake will hit the United States tomorrow. _____

3. Write **likely** or **unlikely** next to each of these statements.

    a. My principal will have long purple hair at school next Monday. _____

    b. It will snow in the middle of summer. _____

    c. The moon will be seen in the evening sky. _____

    d. A dinosaur will sit down at my dinner table. _____

    e. Nobody will wear a seat belt tomorrow. _____

    f. A baby will be born on Friday. _____

#8995 Targeting Math: Geometry, Chance and Data			© Teacher Created Resources, Inc.

Chance and Data

Possible Paths

Name **Date**

1. Look at this diagram of a small theater. Using colored pencils, draw in all the possible paths you can take if you walk from the entrances to the exit.

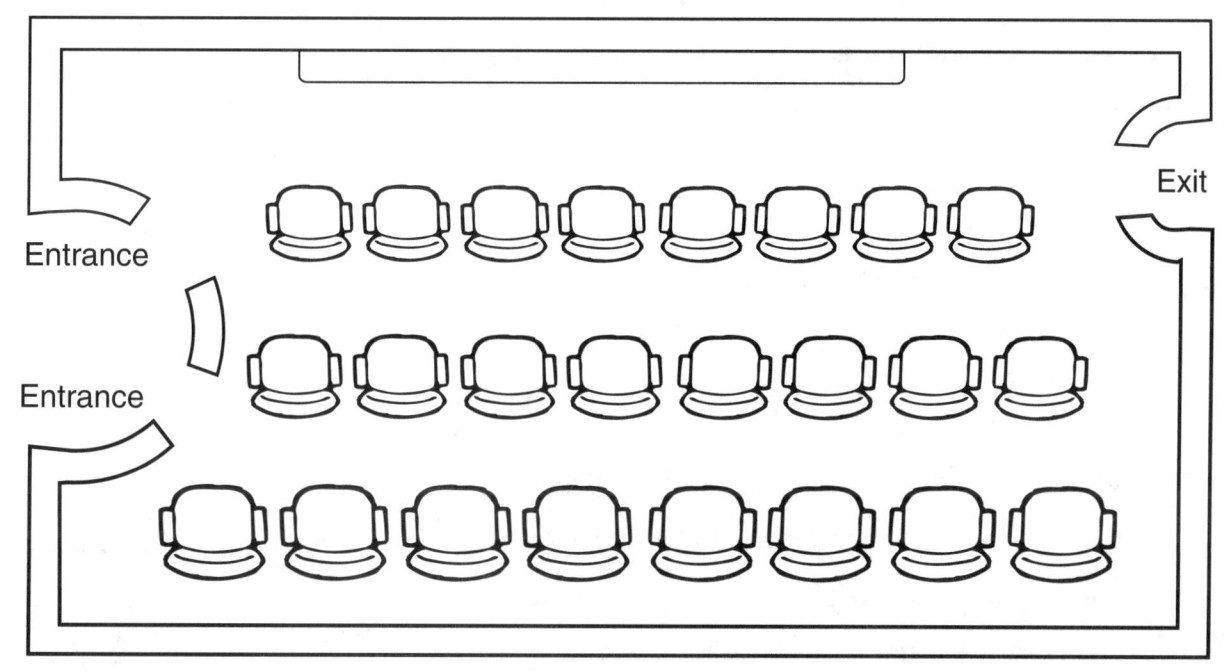

How many different paths did you find? _____

2. This is Uncle Andrew's orchard. Show the different paths that the tractor must follow if it checks for weeds down each row and between each tree.

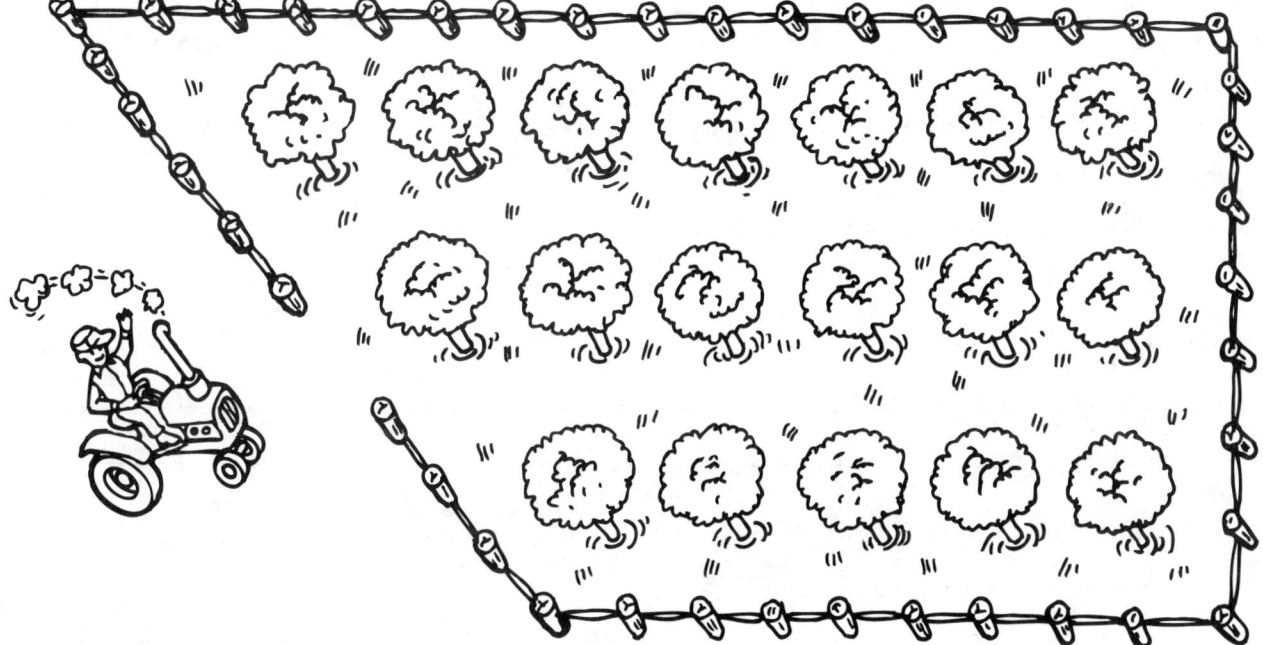

Compare your results with a friend's.

© Teacher Created Resources, Inc. #8995 Targeting Math: Geometry, Chance and Data

Chance and Data   True or False

Name	Date

1. Read the statements below. Write **true**, **false**, or **unsure**.
   a. People will take vacations on the moon. _____
   b. Next year there will be more students in fourth grade than this year. _____
   c. There are 13 months in a leap year. _____
   d. All red cars go faster than white cars. _____
   e. The hour hand is usually the longer hand on an analog clock. _____
   f. Iceland, Switzerland, and Greenland are all countries. _____
   g. There are many different religions in the world. _____
   h. Next year a new type of pen will be invented. _____
   i. There are five Queens in a pack of cards. _____
   j. I will be taller by more than two inches next year. _____
   k. My female cat will have kittens one day. _____
   l. A rabbit can turn into a mouse. _____

2. ⟨ A prediction is something that is likely to happen in the future. ⟩

   For example: I predict that I will wear shoes next week.
   a. Write four predictions of your own.
      I predict _____
      I predict _____
      I predict _____
      I predict _____
   b. Read your predictions to a partner. Write one of his or her predictions.
      My partner predicted _____
      _____
   c. Write a "silly" prediction: _____
   _____

#8995 Targeting Math: Geometry, Chance and Data   © Teacher Created Resources, Inc.

Chance and Data   Being Certain

Name   **Date**

1. Color the balls in the bag so you would be certain to choose a red one.

2. Color the stars so it would be possible to choose two blue stars out of the seven stars.

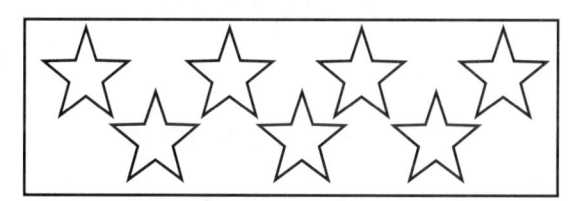

3. Color the flowers so that it would be impossible for you to choose a white one.

4. Color the rectangles so you would have an equal chance of choosing a yellow or a pink one.

5. Color the marbles to show that you would have an equal chance of choosing a black, a green, or a red one.

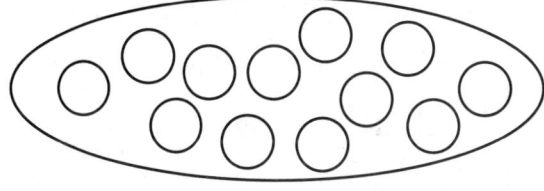

6. Draw and color the pencils so that you would have a 2 in 8 chance of choosing an orange one.

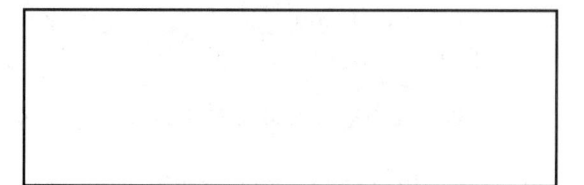

7. Write your own story to match this picture.

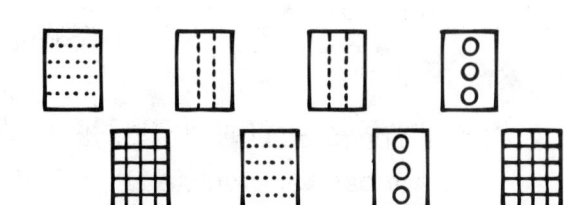

_____
_____
_____

93

© Teacher Created Resources, Inc.   #8995 Targeting Math: Geometry, Chance and Data

Chance and Data   Chances

Name _____   **Date** _____

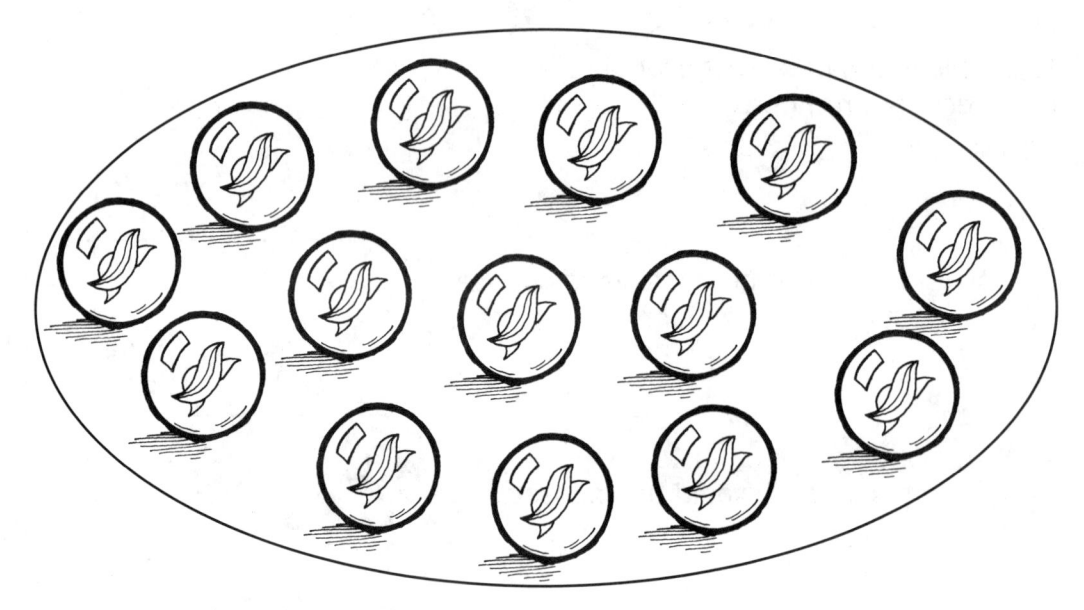

1. There are 14 marbles in the sand pit. One is green.

   > The chances of selecting the green one the first time is 1 in 14. (If you are not looking, of course!)

   If you put the green marble back:

   a. What is the chance of selecting the green marble on the sixth turn?
   _____

   b. What is the chance of selecting the green one when there are only eight marbles left in the sand pit? _____

   c. How many turns must you have to be guaranteed you will choose the green marble?
   _____

   d. Explain why the chance of selecting the green marble changes with each turn.
   _____

   e. Does it become easier or harder to select the green marble after 11 turns?
   _____

   f. How many marbles will remain in the sand pit after the second turn?
   _____

2. Think of some everyday situations that are similar to the above event (e.g., selecting a player for your sports team). List them on the lines below.
   _____
   _____

94

#8995 Targeting Math: Geometry, Chance and Data   © Teacher Created Resources, Inc.

Chance and Data   Choices! Choices!

Name   **Date**

1. List all the different sandwiches you could have if you could choose two fillings from the following options: ham, cheese, tomato, or lettuce. The first one has been done for you.

   a. ____ham and lettuce____   b. _____

   c. _____   d. _____

   e. _____   f. _____

2. Your ice-cream shop has five different flavors of ice-cream, plain cones, and waffle cones. Decide what the five flavors are and make as many ice-cream combinations as possible. List them.

   My flavors are

   1. _____   4. _____
   2. _____   5. _____
   3. _____

   My ice cream combinations are

   _____
   _____
   _____

3. Aunt Jerry works in a pizza shop. Customers can choose from the following:

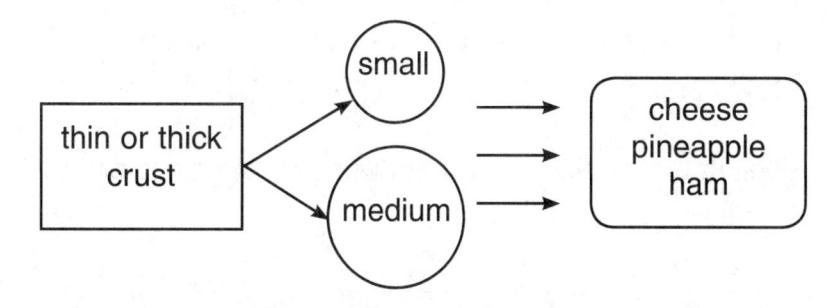

   thin or thick crust → small / medium → cheese, pineapple, ham

   a. Write the number sentence to show the possible combinations.

      ☐ x ☐ x ☐ = ☐

   b. "Large" was added to the selection along with "mushrooms." Write the new number sentence.

      ☐ x ☐ x ☐ = ☐

95

© Teacher Created Resources, Inc.   #8995 Targeting Math: Geometry, Chance and Data

Chance and Data   Assessment

Name | **Date**

1. List two events that are likely or unlikely to happen.
   a. Likely _____
   _____
   b. Unlikely _____
   _____

2. List one possible and one impossible event.
   a. Possible _____
   b. Impossible _____

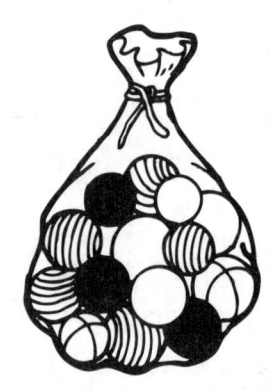

3. What are the chances of:
   a. choosing a black ball? _____ chance(s) in _____ .
   b. choosing a ball marked x? _____ in _____ .
   c. choosing either a white or a striped ball? _____ .
   d. choosing a colored or a patterned ball? _____ .

4. Write the number sentence used to solve:
   a. choices: cheese, nuts, jam or honey on white or brown bread.   ☐ × ☐ = ☐
   b. choices: sandals or sneakers with jeans, shorts or a bathing suit. ☐ × ☐ = ☐
   c. choices: fried or boiled eggs with bacon, ham or sausage with BBQ or tomato sauce.   ☐ × ☐ × ☐ = ☐

5. Make two predictions: one that is likely to happen tomorrow and one that is not.
   a. _____
   b. _____

#8995 Targeting Math: Geometry, Chance and Data   © Teacher Created Resources, Inc.

Activity Page

Name **Date**

Chance and Data

Enlarge the game board to 8 ½" x 11" paper.
Equipment: A die, a coin and a colored counter for each player
Players: 2–4
Aim: To be the first player to get through the maze
To play: Toss the coin and the die. If you get "heads," move forward the number shown on the die. If you get "tails," move backwards the number shown on the die. If you land on a diamond, go back double the number shown on the die for your last throw. If you land on a star, go back to the start. The first person to move his or her counter through the maze is the winner.

If you find yourself at a dead end, you will have to get tails on your next turn to turn around and go back.

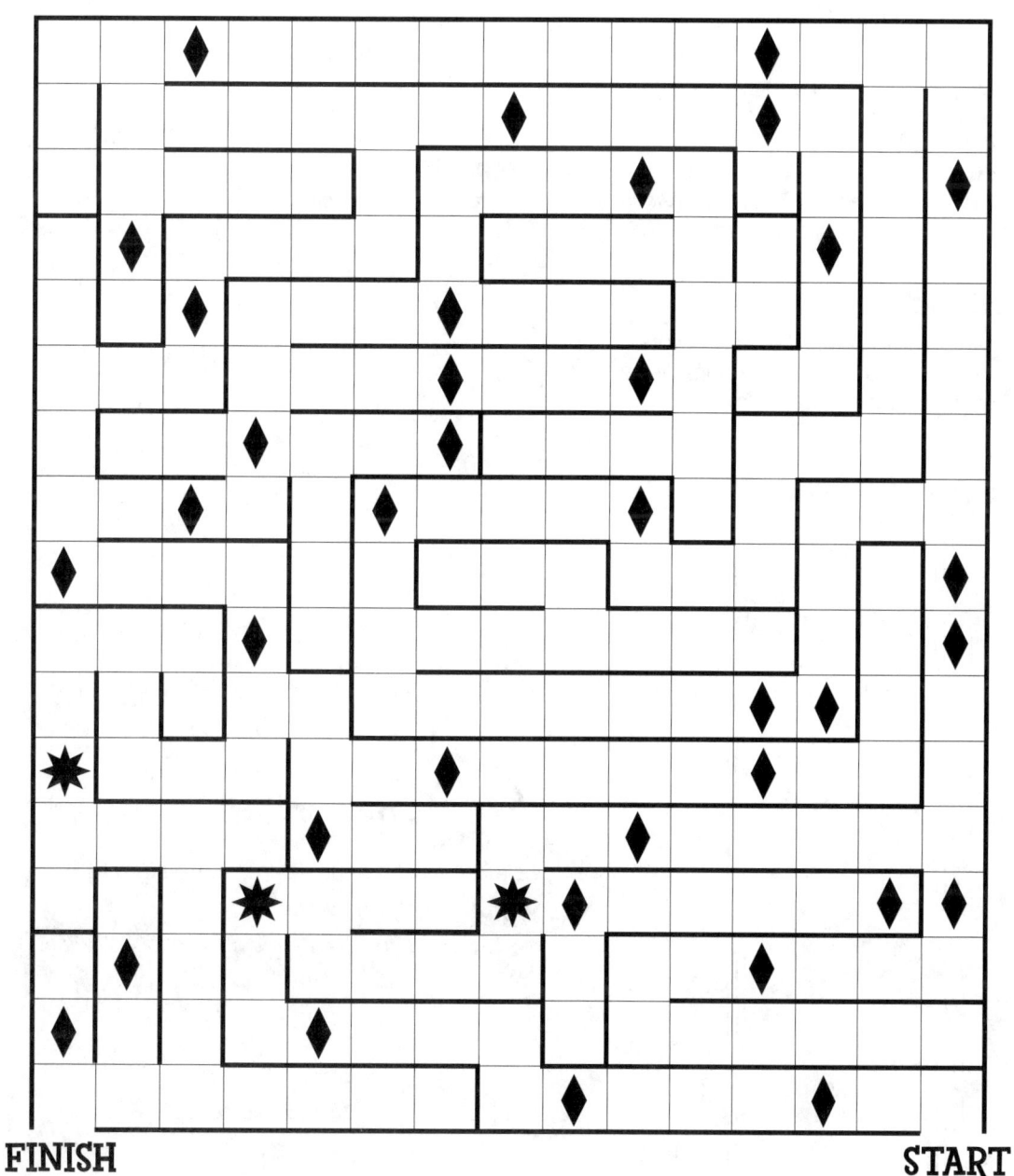

FINISH   START   97

© Teacher Created Resources, Inc.   #8995 Targeting Math: Geometry, Chance and Data

CHANCE AND DATA

Unit 2

*Chance
Probability
Data
Predictions
Ordering
Experiments*

Objectives

- record and identify all possible outcomes arising from simple chance experiments
- consider predictions after data collection
- order events from least likely to most likely
- realize that justification of intuitive insights is important

Language

likely, not likely, chance, predict, prediction, guess, possible, possibility, digit, spinner, record, information, combination, statement

Materials/Resources

unifix blocks (five of each of the following colors: yellow, blue, red, green), dice, paper, rulers, large sheets of paper, colored pencils, coins

Contents of Student Pages

* Materials needed for each reproducible page

Page 100 Funny Faces
use different combinations of given data

Page 101 Most Likely
order events; write own questions

Page 102 Predictions
collect data; record results
* unifix blocks

Page 103 Chance
experiment using dice; predict results
* dice

Page 104 Different Ways
find all possible outcomes; list events with one outcome
* coins, colored pencils

Page 105 Tossing Coins
true or false; write statements; predict outcomes
* coins

Page 106 Assessment
* colored pencils

Remember

Before starting ensure that each student:
☐ checks answers.
☐ reads problem-solving questions twice.

Additional Activities

❏ *Encourage children to justify answers to their peers. The justification process requires an ordering of thoughts and a depth of understanding.*

❏ *Predict outcomes daily for a week. Record predictions and results. (For example, Will it rain tomorrow? Will Mr. Smith wear black shoes on Wednesday? Will more children have an apple or a banana in their lunch on Friday? etc.) At the end of the week discuss results.*

❏ *Many of the activities on student pages can be repeated using different data.*

Page 100—dogs with different ears, tails and collars.

Page 104—finding different paths on maps.

Page 106—use different colored candies in a bag.

Answers

Page 100 Funny Faces
1. Twelve combinations are achievable.
2. Twelve combinations are achievable.

Page 101 Most Likely
Check individual work.

Page 102 Predictions
1–4. Check individual work.
   5. It is easier to guess when you keep a record.
      Easier: The fewer the number of colors.
      Harder: The greater the number of colors.

Page 103 Chance
1. 6, true
2. varies
3. a. 11—2, 3, 4, 5, 6, 7, 8, 9, 10, 11, 12
   b. 5
   c. 5:11, there are 5 chances in 11 to get eight or more.
4. a. 120
   b. 23
   c. 23:130 Can only use number combinations of 256, 346, 356, 436, 456.

Page 104 Different Ways
1. The answers for all questions depend on what the class accepts as an answer. There is great scope for discussion here, i.e., you may only accept
3 x 5c + 10c = 25c
5 x 5c = 25c
2 x 10c + 5c = 25c
1 x 25c = 25c
or you may also accept the order in which they are presented, i.e.,
5c + 5c + 5c + 10c = 25c as different from
5c + 10c + 5c + 5 = 25c
2. Check individual work.
3. Check individual work.

Page 105 Tossing Coins
1. Heads, Tails, True
2. a. Heads, Heads, Heads, Tails, Tails, Heads, Tails, Tails
   b. 4
   c. 1:4, 1:4, 1:4, 1:4
   d. In general: there is one chance in eight of the coins landing as predicted.
3. a. Heads, Heads, Heads
     Heads, Tail, Heads
     Heads, Heads, Tail
     Heads, Tail, Tail
     Tail, Tail, Tail
     Tail, Heads, Tail
     Tail, Tail, Heads
     Tail, Heads, Heads
   b. 8
   c. In general: there is one chance in eight of the coins landing as predicted.
4. 16. In general: there is one chance in sixteen of the coins landing as predicted.
    Heads, Heads, Heads, Heads;
    Heads, Tail, Heads, Heads;
    Heads, Heads, Tail, Heads;
    Heads, Tail, Tail, Heads;
    Heads, Heads, Heads, Tail;
    Heads, Heads, Tail, Tail;
    Tail, Tail, Tail Heads;
    Tail, Heads, Tail, Tail;
    Tail, Tail, Tail, Tail;
    Tail, Heads, Tail, Heads;
    Tail, Tail, Heads, Heads;
    Tail, Heads, Heads, Tail;
    Tail, Heads, Heads, Heads;
    Heads, Tail, Heads, Tail;
    Tail, Tail, Heads, Tail;
    Heads, Tail, Tail, Tail

Page 106 Assessment
1. a. 1:3
   b. 1:2
   c. 1:4
   d. 1:1
2. 12 ways
3. Most likely = c, e
   Likely = a, b
   Not Likely = d, f

© Teacher Created Resources, Inc.   *#8995 Targeting Math: Geometry, Chance and Data*

Chance and Data

Funny Faces

Name   **Date**

1. Try to make twelve different faces by using different combinations of:
   - a happy or a sad mouth; 
   - sunglasses, reading glasses or no glasses; 
   - long hair or short hair.

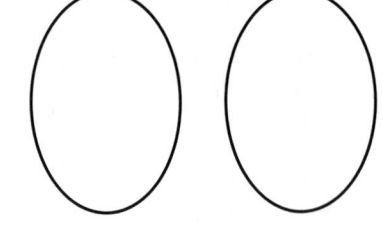

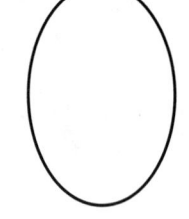

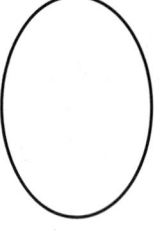

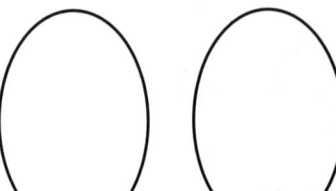

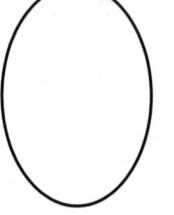

2. Try to make twelve different faces with:
   - glasses or no glasses 
   - a happy or a sad mouth 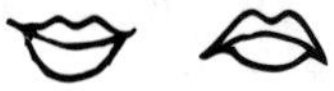
   - no hair, curly hair, or straight hair

#8995 Targeting Math: Geometry, Chance and Data   © Teacher Created Resources, Inc.

Chance and Data   Most Likely

Name   **Date**

1. Check the box which best describes the chance of the sentence being true.

	Most Likely	Likely	Not Likely	
a.	☐	☐	☐	My mother ate three hamburgers for lunch.
b.	☐	☐	☐	Our car has two steering wheels.
c.	☐	☐	☐	This piece of chocolate is made from wood.
d.	☐	☐	☐	I have five sisters.
e.	☐	☐	☐	There are laces in my boots.
f.	☐	☐	☐	We just had toast, eggs, and juice for breakfast.

2. Sometimes we need to know what is happening around us before we can make a prediction. Would your answers change if you had this extra information?

	Most Likely	Likely	Not Likely	
a.	☐	☐	☐	My mother ate three hamburgers for lunch because they were mini hamburgers and she had not had breakfast.
b.	☐	☐	☐	Our car has two steering wheels. One of them is real and the other one is a toy that the baby plays with.
c.	☐	☐	☐	This piece of toy chocolate is made from wood.
d.	☐	☐	☐	I have five sisters and 17 brothers.
e.	☐	☐	☐	There are laces in my pull-on boots.
f.	☐	☐	☐	The electricity was off when we got up so we just had toast, eggs, and juice for breakfast.

Extension: Write some statements like the ones above for a friend to predict. Try to make questions that might change it there was more information. Make sure you have a combination of **Most Likely**, **Likely**, and **Not Likely** answers.

© Teacher Created Resources, Inc.   #8995 Targeting Math: Geometry, Chance and Data

Chance and Data   Predictions

Name   **Date**

1. Place three blue, three yellow, three red and three green Unifix blocks in a box. Without looking, guess each color before taking each block out. Keep a record of your answers in the box below.

✓											
✗											

   How many did you guess correctly? _____

2. Try again.

✓											
✗											

   How many did you guess correctly? _____

3. Try again. This time keep a record of what color comes out as well and think about what colors are left in the box. Hint: Use the information you recorded to help you guess.

Red											
✓											

   How many did you guess correctly this time? _____

4. Again keep a record of the color and use the information to help your next guess.

Red											
✓											

   How many did you guess correctly this time? _____

5. Write a statement about what happens when you record the color as well.

   _____
   _____

Extension: Try with different numbers of each color. Record your results.

What makes predicting easier? _____

What makes predicting harder? _____

#8995 Targeting Math: Geometry, Chance and Data   © Teacher Created Resources, Inc.

Chance and Data   Chance

Name   **Date**

1. When you roll a die the possible answers are

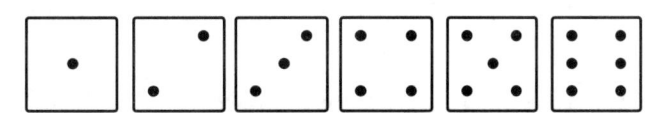

   [die faces 1-6]

   How many possible answers are there? _____
   Statement: When you roll a die your chance of rolling a [die face] is 1 chance out of 6.
   True or False _____

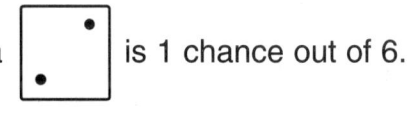

2. Roll two dice together ten times and keep a record of the numbers on each die. After each roll add the two numbers together.

   How often did the numbers add to eight or more? _____

3. Using the two dice:

   a. Add the numbers together to find out how many different answers are possible.
   _____

   b. Predict how many chances of getting eight or more there are. _____

   c. How many ways are there of getting eight? _____

4. Use three dice, with number values instead of dots. Arrange them so there are no numbers repeated.

   a. How many three-digit numbers can you make? _____

   b. Predict how many chances of getting 13 or more there are when the three digits are added together. _____

   c. How many ways are there to make 13? _____

   d. Is this close to what you predicted? _____

5. Try questions from number 4 with four dice.

   a. How many four-digit numbers can you make? _____

   b. Predict how many chances of getting 13 or more there are when the four digits are added together. _____

   c. How many ways are there to make thirteen? _____

   d. Is this close to what you predicted? _____

© Teacher Created Resources, Inc.   #8995 Targeting Math: Geometry, Chance and Data

Chance and Data *Different Ways*

| **Name** | **Date** |

1. Use 5-cent, 10-cent, 25-cent, and 50-cent coins. Circle True or False.

   a. There are more than four ways to make 25 cents. **True or False**

   b. There are more than six different ways to make 30 cents. **True or False**

   c. Show how many different ways there are to make 50 cents.
   (Use the back of this page if you need more space.)

2. Only moving forward, help the puppy find eight different ways to get to her bones. Use a different color for each path.

3. List three true statements that have only one answer. For example, there are always 24 hours in a day.

   a. _____

   b. _____

   c. _____

#8995 Targeting Math: Geometry, Chance and Data © Teacher Created Resources, Inc.

Chance and Data   Tossing Coins

Name   **Date**

1. How many different answers can you get when you toss a coin? Draw your answer on another piece of paper.

   Statement: When tossing a coin there is one chance out of two possibilities that it will land on heads.   **True or False**

2. a. Toss two coins at once. What are the possible combinations? Use as many of the circles below as you need to show each possible answer. Use **H** for heads and **T** for tails. Check to make sure they are all different.

   ○ ○ ○ ○ ○ ○ ○
   ○ ○ ○ ○ ○ ○ ○

   b. How many different answers are possible? _____
   c. What were the chances of tossing 1 heads and 1 tails _____ , 2 heads _____ , 1 tails and 1 heads _____ , 2 tails _____ ?
   d. Write a statement about your findings that describes your chances for landing on different combinations. _____
   _____

3. a. Toss three coins at once. What are all the possible combinations? Use as many of the circles below as you need to show each possible answer. Use **H** for heads and **T** for tails. Check to make sure they are all different.

   ○ ○ ○ ○ ○ ○ ○ ○ ○ ○
   ○ ○ ○ ○ ○ ○ ○ ○ ○ ○
   ○ ○ ○ ○ ○ ○ ○ ○ ○ ○

   b. How many different answers are possible? _____
   c. Write a statement about your findings that describe your chances for landing on different combinations. _____
   _____

4. Predict how many different answers are possible with four coins. Test your predictions with four coins. Look for a pattern in the numbers and use this to help you. On the back of this paper, write a statement about any patterns you notice.

(105)

© Teacher Created Resources, Inc.   #8995 Targeting Math: Geometry, Chance and Data

Chance and Data   Assessment

Name   **Date**

1. Place the following marble combinations in a bag. Then, answer the questions.
   a. 4 red, 4 blue and 4 yellow
      What is your chance of taking out a red marble? _____
   b. 6 red and 6 blue
      What is your chance of taking out a red marble? _____
   c. 3 red, 3 blue, 3 white and 3 yellow
      What is your chance of taking out a red marble? _____
   d. 12 red marbles
      What is your chance of taking out a red marble? _____

2. Using three kinds of paper, two types of ribbons, and two rolls of tape, how many different ways can you wrap a gift? _____

   Use the back of this page to draw your gifts.

3. Place these statements in the squares below, in order of the two most likely to be true, the two likely to be true, and the two least likely to be true.
   a. There are thirty-one days in a month.
   b. The child had peanut butter on his toast for breakfast.
   c. The computer has all twenty-six letters of the alphabet on its keyboard.
   d. Every ambulance has ejector seats.
   e. There are more than fifty seconds in a minute.
   f. Monkeys are the biggest animals of all.

Most Likely			Likely			Least Likely		

Unfolded Figures

The Cube

Name　　　　　　　　　　　　　　　　　　　　　　**Date**

Cut out this unfolded figure. Match tabs to the cube sides and use tape on the sides of the cube to hold the figure together.

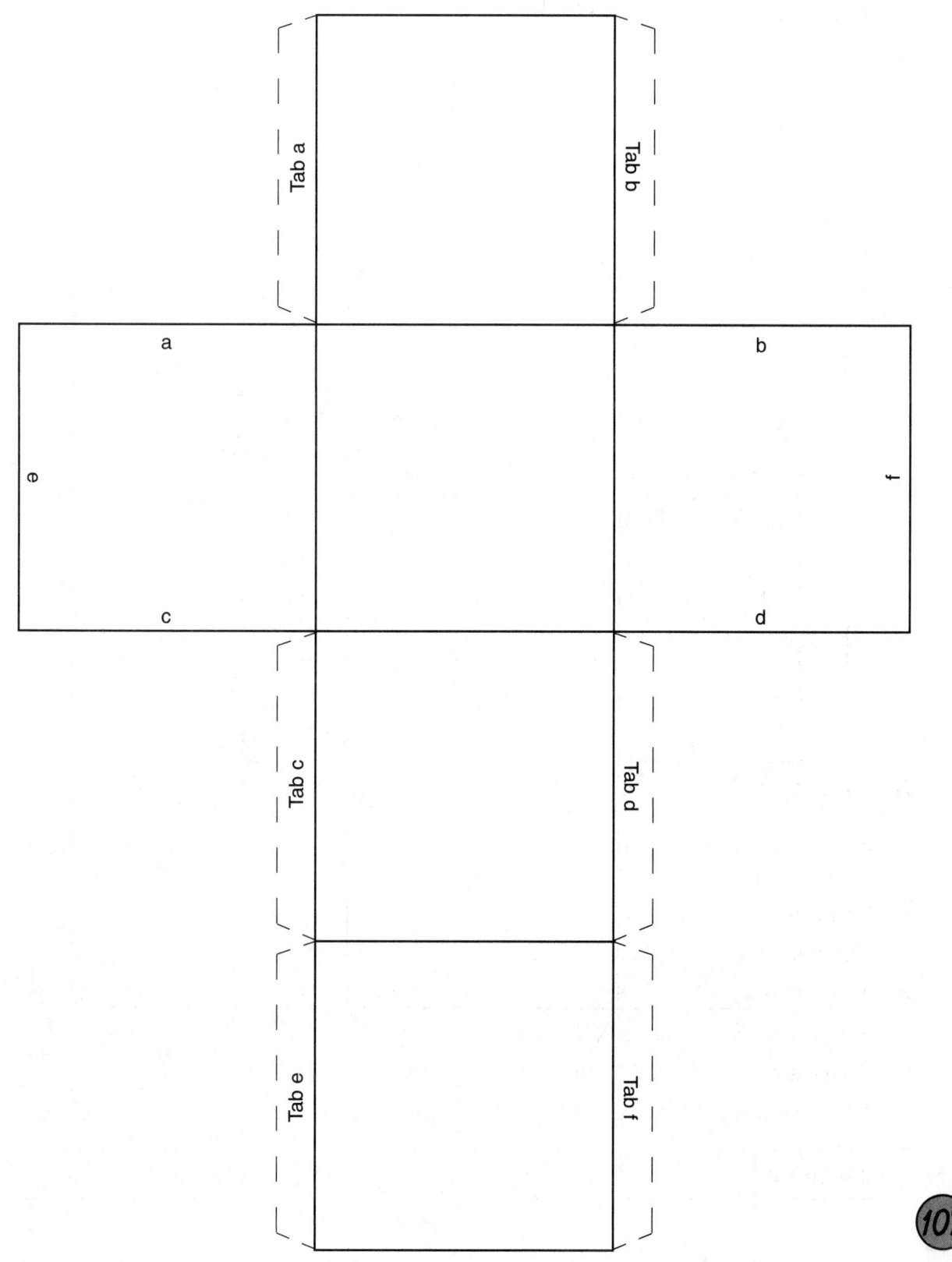

© Teacher Created Resources, Inc.　　　　　　　　　#8995 Targeting Math: Geometry, Chance and Data

Unfolded Figures

The Triangular Prism

Name **Date**

Cut out this unfolded figure, and then fold it on the lines to make a triangular prism. Match tabs to the triangular prism sides and use tape on the sides of the triangular prism to hold the figure together.

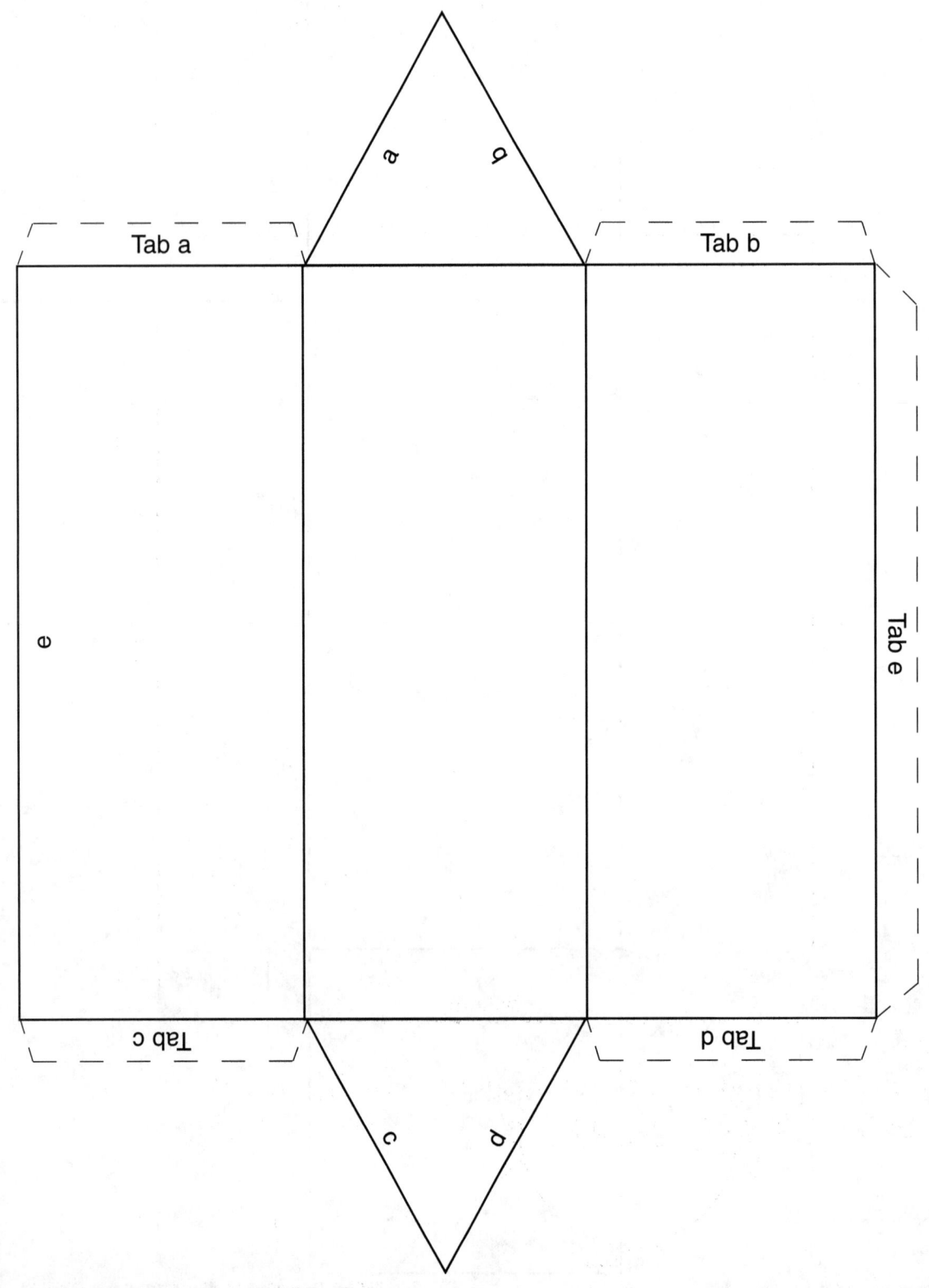

108

#8995 Targeting Math: Geometry, Chance and Data © Teacher Created Resources, Inc.

Unfolded Figures   The Cylinder

Name   **Date**

Cut out this unfolded figure. Attach tab a to side a with tape to form a cylinder shape. Then tape the "top" tabs to the top of the cylinder. Do the same for the cylinder bottom.

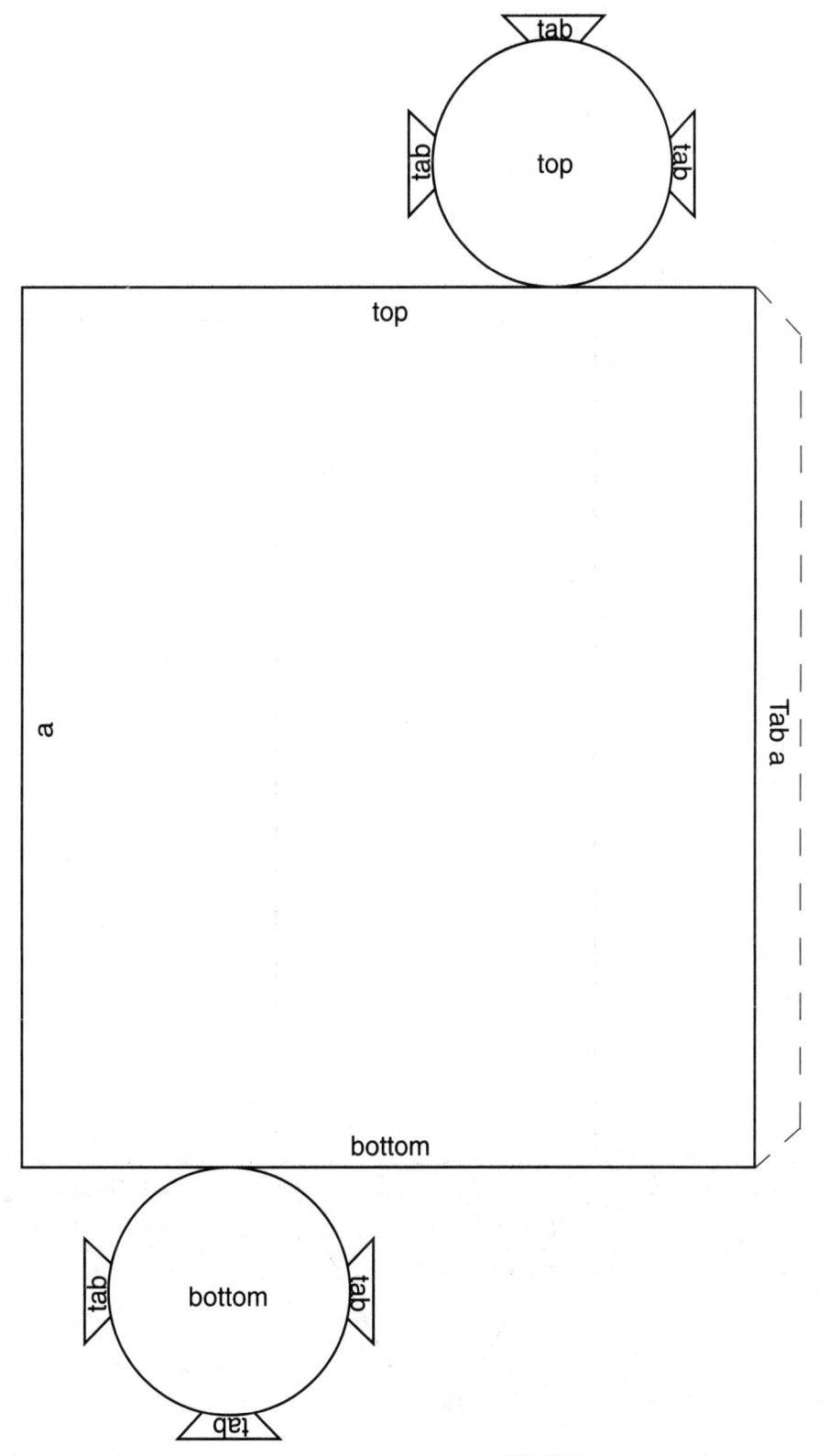

109

© Teacher Created Resources, Inc.   #8995 Targeting Math: Geometry, Chance and Data

Unfolded Figures | The Cone

Name | **Date**

Cut out this unfolded figure. Attach tab a to side a to form the cone base. Then tape the "top" tabs to the cone top.

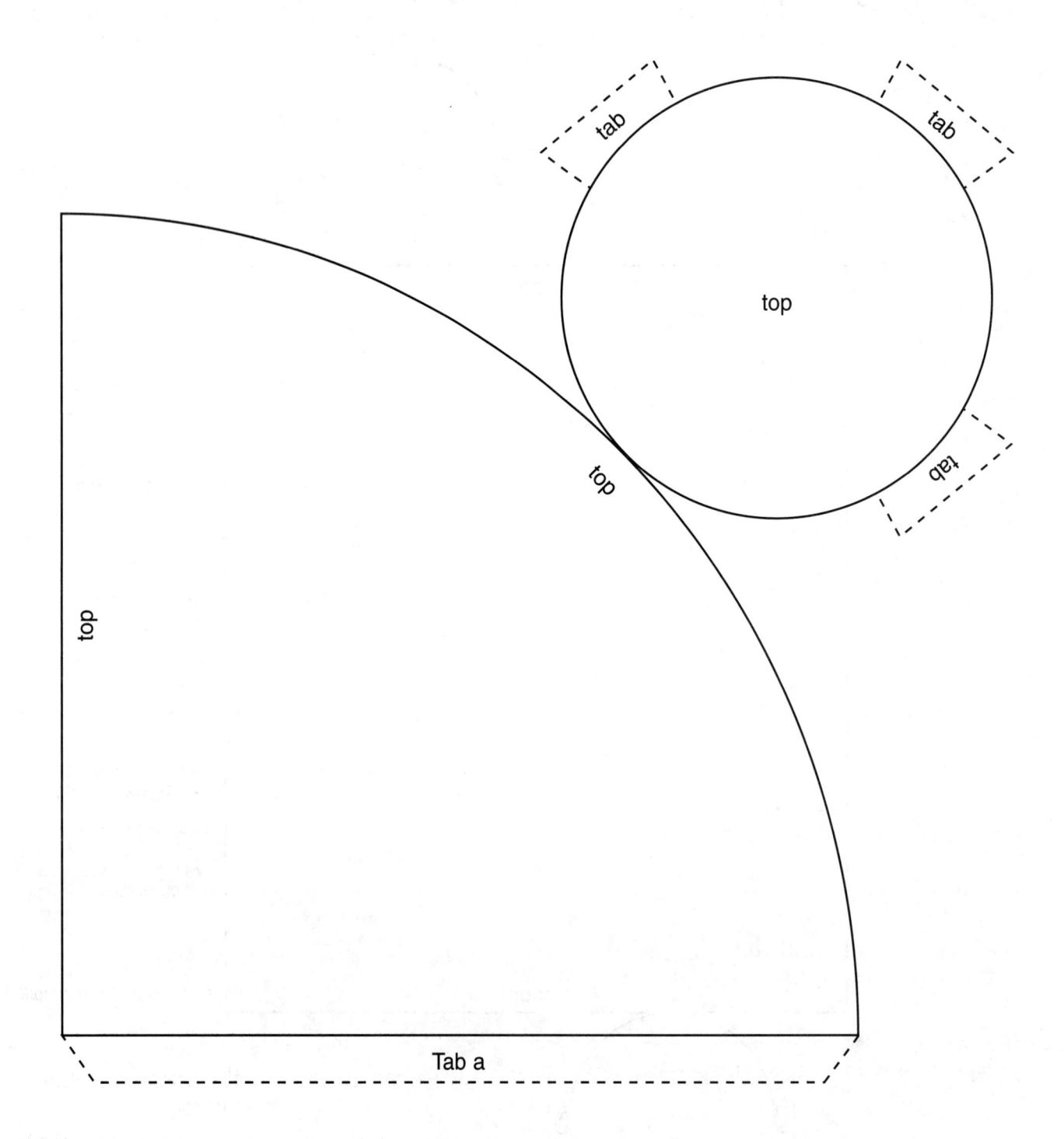

tab

tab

top

top

tab

top

Tab a

110

#8995 Targeting Math: Geometry, Chance and Data © Teacher Created Resources, Inc.

Skills Index

The following index lists specific objectives for the student pages of each unit in the book. The objectives are grouped according to the sections listed in the Table of Contents. Use the Skills Index as a resource for identifying the units and student pages you wish to use.

Two-Dimensional Shapes

make, classify, name, and describe the properties of two-dimensional shapes (Pages: 8, 11, 19)

appreciate the importance of visualization when problem-solving (Pages: 8, 10, 13, 20, 21, 23)

recognize, name, make, and describe the properties of simple two-dimensional shapes using everyday language by observing similarities andt differences (Pages: 9, 11, 18, 22)

demonstrate in practical situations that an angle is an amount of rotation and describe and compare angles using everyday language (Pages: 12, 13, 18, 20)

create tessellations and other patterns (Page: 21)

Three-Dimensional Shapes

identify, compare, classify and construct three-dimensional objects and represent them in drawings (Pages: 28, 41)

describe, model, sort, and recognize three-dimensional objects using everyday language (Pages: 29, 32, 33)

identify and describe prisms and pyramids. (Pages: 30, 39, 42)

describe and compare the spatial features of mathematical objects (Pages: 30, 31, 39, 41, 42)

draw cross-sections of three-dimensional shapes (Page: 40)

match different prisms and pyramids with their unfolded figures (Page: 43)

discuss what is seen and not seen of an object from different positions and represent what is not seen (Pages: 40, 43)

identify, compare, classify, and construct three-dimensional objects and represent them in drawings (Page: 38)

Position and Mapping

describe the position of objects in relation to one another and use simple maps and informal grids to represent this relationship (Page: 48)

use directional language in describing location (Pages: 49, 50)

note order and proximity on maps (Pages: 51, 52, 53)

Transformation and Symmetry

visualize and describe patterns in terms of flipping and sliding (Page: 58)

construct patterns using flips and slides (Page: 63)

construct patterns using flips, slides, and turns (Page: 58)

construct and assemble tangram puzzles. (Page: 59)

make and identify symmetrical patterns. (Pages: 60, 62)

make and identify symmetrical shapes. (Page: 61)

recognize symmetry in the environment. (Page: 60)

Graphs

display, read and interpret a variety of graphs (Pages: 70, 74, 80, 85)

gather, organize, display, and interpret data and present findings in a column graph or bar graph (Pages: 72, 82)

summarize data based on tallying or organized lists (Pages: 70, 71, 75, 81, 83, 84)

check whether answers to problems are correct and sensible (Pages: 73, 84, 85)

Chance and Data

record and identify all possible outcomes arising from simple chance experiments. (Pages: 91, 93, 95, 100, 102, 103, 104, 105)

analyze situations and explain which events are possible, impossible, or certain to occur (Page: 90)

order easily understood events from least likely to most likely (Page: 101)

© Teacher Created Resources, Inc. #8995 Targeting Math: Geometry, Chance and Data

Skills Index

Chance and Data (cont.)

order easily understood events from least likely to most likely and justify choice. (Page: 90)

compare own methods of solutions to problems with those of others. (Pages: 91, 92)

explore different possibilities in familiar situations as an informal introduction to probability concepts (Page: 91)

make simple predictive statements about everyday events using the appropriate language of chance (Page: 92)

predict and validate the outcomes of simple probability experiments (Page: 94)

consider predictions after data collection (Page: 103)

realize that justification of intuitive insights is important (Page: 104)